Set Another Place at the Table

"Company's Coming"

Set Another Place at the Table

"Company's Coming"

by
Sandy Knipp

Mountain Press
Ashland, Kentucky
2005

Dedication

I would want to thank God for all his blessings but especially for finding a kidney for me on March 4, 1999. Every day is a gift. Then to all the guys who are required to come in close contact with me, I apologize, it's not catching. The Kentucky Center for Traditional Music personnel, Jill, Don, Jessee and Toni, "It's not me, it's the computer." My wife, Debbie has a high tolerance level for me and my interests, "Bluegrass music has never hurt anyone." Randy Wells, "Want to sing one more for me?" Harvey Pennington, "That last shot I fired is still traveling somewhere."

Bob, "It's time for a fast fiddle tune." Pastor Ben, "Thanks for all the lessons from the Scripture." Tori, " When you sing, all is right with the world." Johnson First Church of God, Morehead, Tina, "You bless by allowing God to bless you. Was I singing on key last Sunday?"

Introduction

"The Way It Was Then"

I was born during a time of great transition. Folks were signing up for telephone service in their homes. Only two of my friends had telephones during the early sixties and those two parties shared the same line along with as many as six others. There were no private lines out in the country so one party could, and did, listen in on neighbor's conversations. The older rotary-dialed phones took a few seconds to connect with the other person receiving the call. If we needed to make an important call, we would ask permission to use their phone. Although these calls were few and far between, they made for interesting moments when several people gathered close enough to listen to one-sided conversations. Often, someone in the listening audience became curious and offered verbal help and sometimes, even asked questions as to what the other party had said. There were lots of shushings and finger to the mouth sign language to tell a brother or sister or husband to keep quieter. Private phone calls were uncommon.

Aluminum antennae rose from most houses who received one of three available sources of television signals from the sky. Some owners of television sets strung wires that stretched hundreds of yards up hill to try to get a better signal and clear up the "snow" on the screens. Electrical boosters were installed in the homes to make it possible to have a brighter, crisper picture on the black and white receiver screens. At our house, we never enjoyed television because neither dad or mom believed one should own such a luxury. When my brothers and I wanted to watch any television, we walked to my friend Marvin's house. I have often thought how nice our friends had been to my family and how we interfered with that family's privacy during the evenings.

I don't remember ever having been refused a seat for this week's edition of "Bonanza" or "Andy Griffith" but we didn't get to watch that often. The next day at school, I would listen as the children would discuss what happened to their favorite heroes. I wouldn't know about that because I hadn't watched t.v. that night. I have mixed feelings about not having television.

Water froze in the bucket back in the kitchen because the fire in our wood cook stove would go out after supper. Our house wasn't fully plumbed nor was it heated in every room until I was a teenager. Treks to the outhouse during the winter took much less time than those during the summer. One had his business to focus on and didn't dwell too long. This "necessary" room was built so it stretched out over the creek that ran in front of our house and our driveway separated it from our yard. All the stories one hears about outside toilets are true and each person who grew up during this the period of time has one or two good ones to tell.

Set Another Place at the Table

If one has allergies to feathers, he or she need never to sleep on a feather bed. These beds were literally stuffed with the small feathers of duck or chicken and the edges are sewed to keep the contents inside. Used primarily because of their warmth, these beds were not famous for inducing good sleep. I was allergic to feathers then and sometimes I think I was allergic also to my two brothers who slept on either side of me. I kept warm, however. I remember lying awake and debating whether I should make a late-night trip to the outhouse. I might have needed to go badly but climbing up and over one of my brothers, dressing to keep warm for the trip and returning to bed were obstacles I had to learn to overcome. I can imagine the distress from making frequent trips in one night.

The nineteen fifty seven Chevrolet is a classic automobile and debatably the most popular even among car enthusiasts today. I was among the living when the first classic rolled from the assembly line. The fifty eight followed but not with the acceptance and fervor of the previous year's success. My dad traded for a fifty five Chevrolet after having owned a nineteen fifty one Chevy pickup truck. My father drove those automobiles until they needed more repair than was economically feasible. Had we known, we would have kept these old cars and trucks until later and would have been among the classic-car owners group.

These events marked the years of my childhood and they gave to me the experiences and background I cherish so much today. I wouldn't have had it any other way. The story I have written took place directly after these years and the fictitious family I write about didn't exist as any family I knew.

My reasons for writing about these years are to give the readers some time frame for my story and every-day conditions confronting a young child who grew up with me. Things have changed due to the progress brought on by technology. Comic book make believe has come true. I saw the color television with multi-channel capabilities become a commonplace luxury for most all households. Today, telephones can be carried around in our pockets and the use of outhouses is frowned upon. Much later in life, I was fortunate to have owned two classic cars of that time.

Marvin was my closest friend and neighbor. He and I used the many acres owned by our parents as our playground. We spent most of our waking hours together. Limited to the space contained by our two adjoining farms, Marvin and I explored all of it. My first recollections of him involved a ride on a wooden sled filled with new-mown clover hay and pulled by a large black horse. My dad lifted me up onto the tall stack. I can remember the fun we had being pulled along and being jerked forward and falling backward as the horse would speed up and slow down. The ride would end when we would reach the barn and the pile of sweet-smelling hay would be unloaded and stacked in the loft of the barn. There the hay would have lots of time to dry and be fed to this horse and other livestock during the winter months.

Set Another Place at the Table

My childhood buddy and I remained good friends and spent much time together but this story is not so much about our relationship. He was the good neighbor who allowed me to watch his television. Marvin allowed me to accompany him to go in search of the cows which were reluctant to come home to be milked. It was he who was playing with me when the new family came in search of the Marbury place. Marvin and his family kept a respectful distance away from the new family. We never discussed the reasons.

Some of the events and short chapters have some parts that are true. No real names of any persons I knew or know today enter the story. The characters are based loosely and depict the small-world, sheltered life I led. My mother would not allow my brothers, my sister and me to roam any farther than certain landmarks predetermined by her and my father. Other than attending my elementary school, my tracks stayed inside my assigned turf.

It is the interruption of a typical summer day and two children at play that serves as the beginning of my story. I will attempt to paint a picture for you but the picture will be dimmed because I do not have the vocabulary and experience with writing and relating such an unexpected and lasting episode. An appropriate way of beginning may be…"You ain't gonna believe this, but…."

An Old Dodge Truck

Everything they owned was piled on, tied on or held on to the flat bed of a nineteen forty-eight Dodge ton truck. It was the *Beverly Hillbillies* all over again who came to our little world in the summer of nineteen sixty. This scenario keeps coming to mind often during the last fifty years of my life. The event on this day changed my childhood from routine to interesting and makes that time appear even better because of the humor. I can enjoy those times so much easier now. I chose to write about this part of my life before I forgot small details that are memorable and funny yet today. A belly laugh is better than a belly ache, anyday. With this family, brace yourself for one or more per day.

I remember chasing a used tire with a stick while racing to keep up with my childhood friend, Marvin. We were having some troubles getting the dust-filled tires to stop rolling when a big red truck came up our unpaved hollow road and stopped beside my friend's house. "Where's the Marbury place? We're renting the farm now." I pointed toward the dirt-surfaced cemetery road that led up the hill. The driver's name was Burl and he talked while holding a roll-your-own Prince Albert cigarette between his lips from the corner of his mouth. Let me introduce the Marions.

Burl and Mae were parents of nine children. Two older

adolescents seemed very comfortable where they sat with legs dangling over the rear end of the flat bed truck.

These two gentlemen smoked cigarettes and spit onto the ground for the entire time the family spent talking to us that day. Three boys who looked to be the about the same age rode high atop a pile of furniture and smoked cigarettes and constantly spit over the edge of the truck bed. Two young ladies rode while standing and supporting a full-size mattress seemingly trying to keep the bedding upright. They lit up cigarettes while the truck was parked. Another younger lady who appeared to be having problems seeing, sat up front with Burl and Mae. Finally, a youngster who was looking worse for wear was being held in Mae's lap.

I suppose the trance into which I had fallen would have lasted longer had the family mule, also a passenger on the flatbed, not lost his footing when the loud, red truck began to strain under the hard pull of the hill. In retrospect, I can understand the logic of placing a full-size mattress on either side of the animal to help prevent these types of accidents. Maybe the family had the foresight to plan for such mishaps. The family members, all with forty-five mile per hour wind grins, disembarked in the yard of their new home. So, here arrived our neighbors for the next eight years.

From where they came has not been researched but we wondered what living conditions were at their home just before they moved near my family. We asked ourselves questions like, " How did they find out about the Marbury place?"

Set Another Place at the Table

"Why did they choose to rent the farm?" "What were the terms that the Marions and the Marburys agreed upon?" "If living conditions are better here, then how bad were living quarters at their former home?" We never discussed these concerns with anybody outside our immediate family.

Cleanliness

"Cleanliness is next to Godliness." This old saying has been around forever and maybe has biblical grounds to some of us but for some reason cleanliness was not of great importance to the Marion family. My folks, however, lived in an environment practically germ-free and governed to be so by my strong-willed mother. She cleaned our house even when it didn't need cleaning and did so without the luxury of in-house plumbing. Not until I reached the age of fourteen did water run freely from our pipes and fixtures. Sometimes, water froze in the water bucket when left overnight in the kitchen. Yet, we kept clean. Our two worlds clashed when the Marions came to visit. Mom was not a person of tact and was quite free with her advice on many issues.

Whether the topic is morality, theology or procedures for canning green beans, she had her opinions. The five kids living under her roof learned those lessons while still early in life and I consider it a good thing as I roll through the years.

Our doors were always open to everyone, but we lived by Mom's rules. Our neighbors were soon to learn about how to act in "Ola Belle's house."

Supper

Supper at our house was served only after my dad arrived from work, washed and sat down at the table. Only then were we allowed to sit, fully dressed, and eat when we were told. The highest respect for our parents was instilled from birth and continues today long after both my father and mother are gone. In nineteen sixty, behavior was automatic and authority was not questioned within our home. With our neighbors, however, this sort of respect was not a learned practice but knowing when supper was ready to be served was a talent they used frequently. They were never turned away from our table but they learned very soon that to be served, certain rules of table etiquette had to be observed.

Mom was a great teacher and took lots of pride in every facet of homemaking. She worked outside the home only temporarily during a time I was only told about and can't remember. One stern look from her left no room for misunderstanding what was expected. It was this talent that turned a contest for food grabbing into a structured, well-mannered meal. Our friends came often to eat with us at suppertime. Since our supper table had grown, new rules were introduced and old rules were reinforced. Whatever members of the Marion family may have been present for the evening meal learned such things as asking for a specific food to be passed down the table and forks were to be used for transporting food from plate to mouth. We waited for Dad. We wore shirts and even combed our hair. I don't remember anyone going away hungry but I do recall seeing boys going out to play while wearing a shirt they did not have before sitting down to supper with us. Those shirts looked familiar and most of the time they were returned so mom could wash them.

Turf Wars

My second memory of these years involves the coming of the three younger neighbor boys with two of their dogs, Janie and Turk. Our family dog, Scotia, had always protected his turf from skunks, birds, cats and other dogs that strayed too close to his little world. Today, he seemed all too anxious to dive under the porch when he saw the entourage coming up our drive. Scotia was in no hurry to get acquainted. These two new canines-on-the-block ignored the turf lines and helped themselves to our dog's food dish, carrying the dish with its contents out into the yard to finish their meal. Even then, the Marion's two dogs engaged in a bitter quarrel and ensuing fight over rights to my dog's bowl of food. Dog tempers flared and teeth were bared as they stood nose to nose.

Finally, as if on cue, both combatants dropped their war stances and started eating. I still find it amazing after all these years when I think of the audacity and lack of respect shown by our neighbor's dogs.

Haircuts

Try as I may, I cannot call all the Marion children by name, nor can I arrange them in order of birth and according to age. I am always leaving out one or more of them when trying to recall and match a face with a name. One of the ways I use as a memory device is to picture my dad standing behind our green rocking chair with a pair of electric clippers in his right hand. Then, I can remember seeing each of the children sitting down to receive one of dad's patented, one-cut-serves-all haircuts. Nobody complained when one side of a child's head didn't quite match the other. Dad didn't charge for the cuts but expected all the young gentlemen to return monthly for the appointment. I learned that many childhood diseases are prevented by close, scalp-revealing haircuts and that hair usually grows back after a while.

Farming

Early spring brought the smell of burning wood to eastern Kentucky. All the members of the new family knew how to plow, harness a mule, plant seeds and care for their main cash crop, burley tobacco. Farmers would prepare tobacco seed beds by piling scrap wood and setting fire to it. This killed weed seed and made a fertile place for sowing the minute burley tobacco seeds. A cover of white cotton cloth was applied to keep the hot sun from the hundreds of tiny plants that grew from this carefully nurtured area. Mysteriously, the innate urge to clear the fields and prepare the soil led many farmers to feel the need for setting fires to burn lingering plant life left over from last year's crops. On one occasion, a southerly wind whipped the neighbor's fire out of control and burned several acres of the Daniel Boyd National Forest before it was brought under control. While my brothers and I worked with yard rakes, shovels and whatever tools we could find to keep the fire from burning our house and possessions, our new farmer friends took shelter from their observation post. While we worked and sweated and were being covered with black ash from head to toe, our friends stood on their porch and watched the fire burn out of sight.

Farming was a necessary way of life for our new neighbors.

Set Another Place at the Table

They worked at their jobs like ants from an ant hill and got much work done. When gardens began to show results, they were eager to show the product of their hard work and seemed pleased to present my mom with early vegetables. In return for this good deed, she would invite them to share when mealtime came. Burl and Mae brought greens, new potatoes, onions and corn-on-the-cob to our house in paper bags. While each of these vegetables was being prepared, discussions were held as to the correct name of this flower and which wild green was the tastiest and which apples made the best sauce.

Canning and preserving the garden items took much time but assured the family that they wouldn't go hungry during the coming winter. Mae and my mother worked side by side as they peeled, pared, sliced, diced and boiled the vegetables and fruits. Mom supplied the know-how and Burl and Mae supplied the product. Some of the children helped while mom kept a cautious eye on what was being done. The fire that heated the number-three-sized galvanized tub had to be kept burning for hours. The two ladies were well aware of the need to be clean if the canned goods and glass jars were to "keep" for a long time. The Marions shared the results with my family.

Little Josiah sat and watched quietly as his family and my mom worked hard with these chores. His brothers and sisters were constantly talking to him and giving him attention. He seemed to enjoy eating the food they stuck

Set Another Place at the Table

into his mouth each time they passed by. Any of the members of his family changed his diaper when they found it necessary. His eyes would brighten when the top of a canning jar would seal. He slept most of the time, however.

Brickyard Elementary School

Our school was a former high school with hollow halls and high ceilings. The cafeteria was on the south end and the gymnasium on the north. Grades one through eight occupied the spacious building during the years of my early education.

The community surrounding the school was once bustling with manufacturing. As the number of jobs dwindled, the population left to find employment elsewhere.

School started in late August and the job of corralling each of the Marion children into age-appropriate classrooms was a chore taking most of the morning that first day. Our principal's name was Mr. Brach. He assisted in this morning project and the task was completed after a while. Teachers for the most part were modest and used tact when dealing with problematic situations. Having spent many years of my life as an educator, I learned that the majority of problems dealing with educating children have been addressed and solutions are chosen and matched to fit the problem. On this day, nine problems needed nine solutions. Mr. Brach's office was used as a "holding" place until all things were complete. The process went amazingly smooth.

Earsel, Willie and Robert were left handed. The latter two boys ended up in the same seventh-grade class. Sue and Iris had only one dress each. Josiah was not toilet trained.

Oather was seventeen years old. Rosey was almost blind and didn't know it. Blythe had cut his foot on a piece of glass while walking to school that morning. All the children needed new shoes. I can't remember the names of two older children who decided it wasn't worth the effort to walk to school and chose to go squirrel hunting.

In nineteen sixty, a lady named Dochia had the job of head cook at our elementary school. In my opinion, no better meals were ever served and with more pride than those served in the lunchroom where I attended grade school. Of particular importance and most vivid in my memory was chili day. It was usually served on Friday after having served hotdogs on Thursday after having served meat loaf on Wednesday.

This assured the cooks that no hamburger meat would spoil nor be left out to be thrown away. This meal usually consisted of chili, cherry pie and a cheese or peanut butter sandwich. Our cook, Dochia, had the heart of an angel and many times I saw her wrap an extra sandwich with aluminum foil or sandwich wrap and sneak it to the waiting hands of one or more of the Marion children.

Oather, seventeen and rather large and gangly looking in his overalls, was more than happy to help with the garbage detail after everyone had eaten and had gone outside for recess period. Garbage cans were taken outside the school and placed beside the coal-burning furnace room which was located behind the school. Some of the students who were playing on the playground would peek around the corner to watch Oather roll a paper cigarette between his fingers and light up to enjoy a smoke before returning to class.

Classroom Antics

If I made a list of the top twenty mischievous acts that elementary children do to get attention, all would have been performed by those in my seventh grade room. Most always, these dastardly deeds are done by very few of the pupils. I further believe Willie and Robert committed all of them and guilty of thinking even more. They seemed to crave attention and wore perpetual grins on their faces that led one to suspect that the guilt lay with them.

Our teacher, Mr. Essington, began his career by inheriting my class. Years later he told me in private that the remaining twenty-nine of his teaching years were "a piece of cake". He was confronted by various genres of misbehavior that prepared him for whatever may happen in future years of teaching. By having our class to instruct, he learned how students think, react and misbehave. Mr. Essington succeeded in changing the attitudes of a classroom full of boys and girls and most of his students acquired the highest regard for him professionally and personally.

Our rooms had old-fashioned slate blackboards. They served well for pupils to show their work and what they had learned. A few of the students walked up to the board to solve math problems while the others remained in their seats. It just wasn't a complete day unless one of the Marion brothers pelted someone with a chalk-filled eraser. Their day was not fulfilled unless fingernails were scraped across the board to make an irritating sound. Even if they successfully completed their assigned math problem, they left the board having drawn a face with eyes and a tongue sticking out. The chalk figure usually had a classmate's name associated with it. A broken piece of white chalk could be later used as a weapon when hurled across the room at another child. Students were required to erase their board work before returning to his or her assigned seat. This was in essence reloading the "gun" so the eraser could be fired again.

Picture, if you will, the "Joker" character in the movie, "*Batman*" emerging from a cloud of white chalk dust. His painted-on smile would describe Willie or Robert as they returned to their seats and sporting their shades of hair color and those guilty grins. Those two guys breathed enough white chalk dust to coat the insides of their lungs. Most of the time, they took the scenic route when coming back to sit down. The window shades probably needed adjusting so they were more than happy to walk by and tug at the strings used to raise or lower the shades and let them fall. The shades would come crashing down to their full length. Both boys spit a lot and chalk dust seemed to encourage that habit as they approached the waste paper can. Girls were a target for Willie's affections. Julie shrank in fear when he walked by her desk. Chances were very good that he touched her hair or told her he loved her.

Student desks were not bolted to the floor and could be moved by scooting your feet and pushing yourself in any direction. Fingers were pinched, pencils were broken, pigtails were caught and clothes were damaged when one desk was rammed into another. The action reminded one of "bumper cars" at a theme park. The room would be in such disarray that finding one's own desk required a thorough search of the contents of each seat.

The reader should be reminded of the students in the classroom who did not take part in such antics. *We* stood safely away from the action and silently prayed for the quick return of our teacher so the chaos would cease. We learned how to duck when an eraser or a paper wad came flying our way. If someone had to get hit, we shoved Ernie in front of our little group to shield us from the flying missiles. Our room had a small quantity of chalk to disappear each day and it would seem we were tirelessly working away at chalk board lessons. Actually, the overall pants that the two Marion boys wore each day were designed with several pockets of various sizes.

It wasn't actually thieving when chalk was taken home inside these pockets. Some of it came back the next day in the same pocket. Earlier in the story I mentioned my familiarity with Willie's overall pants.

I was not immune to the punishment dished out by the two Marion boys. Although we walked home together and spent countless hours building forts and designing bridges across the streams and playing hide and seek in the barn loft, I was sometimes the target of some of their mischief. I took the abuse for a while but waited for my turn to pay them back. When returning the deeds, or misdeeds if one wants to be specific, the effects can be multiples of the cause. So it was in one case for me. I wanted to pay back doubly.

One day after I had walked home from school, my mother asked me why my hair and shirt collar was so white. She inspected it and found that chalk dust had been poured down the back of my shirt. She wondered how so much of it could have gotten there by accident. I couldn't remember just when Willie had cleaned the chalk tray and emptied the entire day's work down my back. (That much chalk must have been the "after math" of a school day.) Mom made me go outside and take my shirt off so I could clean up. "Chalk one up for Willie".

I carried this episode inside my head for days and waited for just the right moment to even the score. My biggest fear was getting caught and punished by Mr. Essington. I had seen him apply corporal punishment to several boys before. I feared his wrath. I was in no hurry.

Lunch was Willie's favorite time of day. Not only did he enjoy everything on the menu but he and his brother relished the fact that teachers usually did not sit with us in the cafeteria. It was not uncommon for either of the boys to steal food from your plate when you were not looking. Often, I had seen the two boys grab a hamburger or barbeque sandwich from another student's plate and stuff that item of food down into one of those front overall pockets. They would eat it later while walking home or during play time after lunch. Today was Wednesday and it was hamburger day at Brickyard Elementary.

The two Marion boys had sprayed water on some of us while washing up for lunchtime and peeked inside the stall while someone was using the facility and held the bathroom door shut so no one else could get out and messed up another boy's hair within two minutes. We walked on down to the lunchroom. I stayed far behind when we lined up in the hallway and hoped that today I wouldn't have to sit by either one of those guys because I liked hamburgers and I intended to eat all of my own. Willie sought me out and plopped himself down beside me at my table while grinning like a possum in a pawpaw patch.

Caution is a trait I have always used generously but on this day, I threw it into the wind and it disseminated into worthless molecules of nothingness. Dochia, our cook had left the pepper and salt shakers on the table for us to spice up our hamburgers. Willie had cased out the place and had left his seat next to me and had gone to find an unfortunate individual from whom he could snatch yet another sandwich. While he was gone to the other table, I raised up the top bun from his burger and emptied most of the contents of the pepper shaker onto his patty and covered it with his pickles. Mr. Essington entered the cafeteria in time to catch Willie trying to score again. He was asked to return to his seat and eat his own food. While neither the teacher nor Willie knew what was to come next, I did. Mr. Essington wept tears from underneath his glasses while he watched the hamburger snatcher wipe tears caused by eating the hottest hamburger ever prepared at Brickyard Elementary. I felt like applauding. Willie needed some water.

The Rodeo

Willie Marion got a lot of life from a pair of overalls. He was the child closest in age to my own and was in seventh grade with me. I had memorized the tag on the back of those pants because he sat in front of me every day in class. I remember talking to my mom about this and she informed me that things like that were of no concern to me. Actually, to beg to differ with mom, after a week the smell became a dire concern of mine. I tried to think of ways to bring up the topic to Willie and get him to see the necessity to wash his clothes. I can't remember just how this problem was corrected but I believe our teacher said or did something about it.

Corporal punishment was legal during those years and for several years to come. It wasn't until after I became a principal that the practice was abolished. Teachers were to use this type of punishment only as a last resort but it could be used and for the most part, without repercussions from the child's parents. On one particular day, Willie used profanity to express how he felt about getting up in front of class and giving a book report. He offered no excuses but just refused to deliver his oral report and accentuated his refusal with expletives. Our teacher found this type of language offensive and unacceptable and began to lecture this student about the use of those types of words. Willie stunned the entire class when he used it again with much more vigor. His overall pants were not enough to pad the part of his posterior to which Mr. Essington lay on the punishment. I felt like applauding. I do believe the punishment was too severe for the crime but Willie had a better command and control of the English language and his book reports reflected improvement.

During these years, my brothers, my sister and I could either walk a half mile to the end of our road and ride the school bus or walk over the hill to Brickyard Elementary. I enjoyed walking, especially when my brother and I looked for Indian arrowheads in the freshly-plowed tobacco field. The promise of a warm day in early October was reason enough to choose to walk to school. My two older brothers were required to wait a few minutes at my school until they could board the bus bound for the high school. If the weather was not particularly cold or rainy, we chose to start early and take the scenic route past the cemetery, through a field we called "Jake's Field" and down the road to the school. "Jake" was an older man who owned two mules and because of his age, rarely worked the two animals. On mornings like these, the two mules would see us approaching the low place in the barbed wire fence used for crossing over and come to meet us. Maybe they were glad to see a group of happy kids or possibly expecting us to provide some food but I felt scared to be close to the animals.

This latter route took us past the Marion's house and meant

we would pick up several of the neighbor children who chose to walk with us. As I stated earlier, either of them could put a harness on any four-footed animal and plow a straight furrow through a new ground and do so with authority. A number of them joined us to form a crude sort of follow-the-leader procession while headed for school. It was their familiarity with work animals that prompted some of the boys to boast about showing the rest of us how to "handle" Jake's mules. As we approached the section of fence that sagged lower than the rest, the older kids lifted the younger ones over. The two animals came to meet us. Oather thought a little morning mule ride through the pasture was just what the poor animals needed. His brothers agreed and he and Willie each chose an animal they planned to ride.

Mules have never been accused of being too smart. However, they have existed for ages and ages and even prospered. I had not given them enough credit. I want to offer my appreciation to Jake's mules for providing one of the funniest moments in my life. Fewer memories made such a deep wrinkle on my brain as did the rodeo we witnessed that morning in "Jake's Field" while the audience got to watch for free. Oather didn't last for the mandatory eight-second ride. Most of his morning jaunt consisted of his clinging on to the side of his mount while being scraped against a sourwood sapling. Willie fared some better. He was atop his bucking brute just yahoooing and whooopieing like a real pro until his ride came to an end. His mule tired of such sport and lowered its head while raising its behind and the overall pants of the rider caught on the barbed wire as he sailed back over the fence. Willie walked along very quietly and didn't add much to our conversations as we continued on to school.

Physical Education Class

Physical education class at Brickyard Elementary was taught by Bob. Nobody dared call him by that name. A former drill Sargent in the army, Mr. Bob expected everyone to toe the line and never question his authority. He kept the gymnasium floor cleaner than a hospital operating room. He also expected, demanded and got the same respect from his students because he knew how to discipline. I personally feared this man and would have done anything he asked.

The Marion children had no gym shoes to wear and street shoes were never to be worn on the sacred floor so they watched for a couple of days from their seats on the bleachers. Soon, all the children were sporting a new pair of shoes that could be worn in the gym. No one knew that these shoes were donated by a church leader who owned a shoe store in town.

On Fridays, we took our sweaty gym shoes home to be washed along with our sport socks. On Monday during physical education class, Mr. Bob inspected all shoes as the students toed the line while standing on an assigned spot during roll call. The majority of the Marion children followed directions and usually brought back both shoes relatively clean. Not all went well on Monday morning during class, however.

Set Another Place at the Table

Basketball was big in nineteen sixty. Even in grades one through eight, competition was furious among the six elementary schools in our county and during basketball season, each school fielded an "A" team and a "B" team. A school day was used for these competitive games and an entire afternoon was taken to play two games against the other school. Three Marion boys joined the team.

Having never played the sport of basketball before, those three boys had a lot of basic, fundamental sport to learn quickly. Rules had to be explained as the game went along. Much punishment was dished out by the boys as they failed to control their body movements and fouled the other team considerably rougher than expected. Our team may have lost the game by points, but the other team felt beaten after the game.

Puberty had made a mess of the equilibrium of a seventeen year old lad. Walking behind a turning plow over rough terrain came naturally for him. Playing organized sports was not so natural and became so embarrassing that coach Bob stopped insisting that Oather take part in activities that took a lot of coordination. Later that year, the lanky lad was awarded first place in the long jump and the mile run while participating in the elementary school track meet. Unfortunately, the fame was short lived. When he turned eighteen, he left school and found a job working in a foundry in Crestline, Ohio.

Commodity Cheese, Government Give-a-ways & Bootleggers

Cheese came wrapped in plastic and the huge chunks weighed five-pounds each. Round, metal containers held beef that had been sealed in suspension with its own broth. One needed to rise and shine and be first in line on Tuesdays and Thursdays for the dispensing of these food products. One needed only to present his or her card and the rest was done for you. Families planned the day around their trip to the county court house to pick up their allotment. The Marion family was very aware of this program and fared well. Given the number of children in the family, they carried large quantities of the product back to the red Dodge truck.

This program continued for a few years and families who qualified for this assistance should never have gone hungry. Along with an allotment for powdered milk, butter and navy beans, a tasty, balanced meal could be had at the expense of the government. The concept was good and lower income families ate well if they chose to participate in the program. As with many other well-intended subsidies, this program had its down side also. It should not be assumed that everyone has the same intentions for implementing programs such as this one and that all who do take part follow the rules and well-meaning directions for use of these fine food products.

Set Another Place at the Table

Our neighbors adapted to most situations by using their talent for shrewdness. If there was a loophole in the law, they found it. If there was another way to get from point "A" to point "B" with less resistance, they followed it. One such business in our community helped folks like the Marions with acquiring a much sought-after commodity, alcohol.

If a crow flew over our house and continued in a straight line southeast, it would fly near a small wooden structure that sits conveniently by a well-traveled, asphalt backroad. Sitting squarely on the line that separates one county from another, the building served as a place one could purchase alcoholic beverages. Although both counties were "dry" and it was illegal to sell any alcohol, the law was relatively ignored. Trucks carrying beer, wine and whiskey of many varieties made daily trips to a city fifty miles away to buy large quantities of the beverages and bring them back to this building to be sold at marked-up prices. Motorists drove from neighboring counties and pulled around to the back of the building where a friendly salesperson took their order and handed the purchase out the window to them. This business was called "bootlegging".

I understand that sometimes a purchaser may be short of cash and that other items may be used for the transactions at this bootlegger. It was known that a five-pound hunk of cheese had certain value toward the barter for a six pack of beer. I never understood the exchange value of commodity products for alcohol but the Marions knew. They stopped at this beer shack before returning home on Tuesdays and Thursdays. I also do not know how some of the beef and much of the cheese and butter ended up in our refrigerator. It could have been some arrangement between my mother and the Marions but the agreement must have been as binding as the cheese.

The Preacher Comes

If you were alive and breathing on your own and you lived in my house, you went to church on Sunday mornings. The church that my family attended was a little different than some others around the area. It may be interesting to know that we didn't have meetings in the same physical houses every Sunday. We shared the privilege to host the event with other communities. Our regular meeting time was ten o'clock on the first Sunday of each month. Another church house a few miles away would have the honor the next week. A month of Sundays would have our family traveling to four or five different towns in Eastern Kentucky. The same faces would show up to attend but in a different location. This group of churches with the same beliefs and practices was called an "Association". Each year everybody got together and held a large meeting. This event brought many people together for a business meeting and lots of singing and preaching. The culmination of all these activities was held under a huge tent. One year, our church hosted the "Association" and the event took place less than two miles from my house.

Folks like me took in all the sights, sounds and treats at the associations. Occasionally, I would sit through a complete sermon but other things drew my attention away from the church meeting. For instance, a driver of an automobile was having trouble finding a parking place far out in the grass field and the motion of his car attracted my thoughts. I got up from my seat on the wooden bench and sauntered over to where the other action was taking place. This was far more interesting to a youngster my age so I stayed to help. It had rained a small amount the night before and the grassy surface was too slick for the green automobile to get enough traction.

I thought it to be wonderful when I saw those rear tires spin around and around without going anywhere. When the spinning would stop for a moment, I could read the word, "Studebaker" on the inside of the hubcap on the rear tire. The driver was getting impatient and the tires were sinking deeper and deeper. That's when three of the Marion boys walked over to see me.

They had never been to church with me, but the timing couldn't have been better. When they asked what was going on, I told them that this man was a preacher and he needed someone to help push his car forward so he could park. Immediately three over-zealous, overall-clad young men found a spot on the rear of this man's car and began to push. The driver opened the throttle on his engine and the mud slinging began. The car did make some slow progress forward and eventually found a spot between two other vehicles and stopped.

One of the three Marion boys escaped being coated from head to foot with black mud. However, the two guys who found a spot to push the car directly behind the spinning rear tires were not so lucky. Each of the boys had a strip of mud reaching from their feet, up their legs, across their chest and finishing with cheek, ears and hair. It appeared they had turned their heads to escape the mud sling but were defenseless to protect their faces. They were using their hands to hold on to something so they could push the car.

Outdoor church meetings lasted a long time when I was younger. Sometimes, it was approaching two o'clock in the afternoon when the sisters of the church spread the meal on the long tables. Still, it was proper decorum for the elder brothers of the church to be served first. After a prayer of thanks for just about everything made during the first six days on earth, the line would start to move forward toward the "dinner-on-the-grounds". The Marion boys had never been to one of our meetings and the effort exerted while pushing the vehicle that morning had left them hungry. They moved to the front of the line. My mother met them there. Mom was cutting an angel food cake with a long kitchen knife. She said a lot without saying anything at all. The boys came back with me and took a place in line.

Nobody said anything publicly about the three young lads whose pants looked like they had been run over by a tractor tire. Looks of wonderment were cast from many curious eyes toward the boys who wore their new coat of drying mud from head to toe. Everybody ate well.

Sunday was the Lord's day and our church made the best

of it. Well after the day's sermons had been preached and the songs had been lined and sung, the preacher followed us home and came to supper. So did some members of the Marion family who were curious about all the events of the day. They were most interested in a green, Studebaker automobile that was parked at our house that evening. The car wore the state of Ohio license tags. This was the car that covered them with mud this morning. The mud had dried and having company from another state was just too much for the three Marion boys to comprehend. This was possibly the only time that seeing unfamiliar company meant more than eating supper at our house.

"Uncle Bill" had a gift for being able to reach young people and their interests. He asked all the young folk to follow him to his car. From his trunk, he took two sticks, each about a yard long, and whose ends were tied with a section of twine string. He held the sticks parallel with the ground so the length of string would loop near his feet. On the string, he placed a short, wooden section whose center had been whittled away to look like an hour glass. He flipped the string and the whirling piece of wood whizzed and turned very fast. Uncle Bill would throw the wooden piece high up in the air and catch it on the string and do it all over again. We each had a turn at this gizmo. Willie, Robert and Earsel were thoroughly entertained.

Alcohol in My Coke

One summer on the fourth of July, the Marions decided to go all out and celebrate Independence Day with as much gusto as they could afford. The older boys had gotten jobs at the sawmill and more money was coming home. Fireworks were at the top of the list for things to buy for the day-long celebration. Alcohol was also given a lot of importance and ran a close second. The boss down at the mill had given the entire crew the day off and had shut down operations until Monday morning.

Alcohol comes in many forms. Manufacturers can bottle their product or seal it in cans. Then there are those other distillers who escape paying taxes to the government and hide their operations deep inside the ravines and caves found in Eastern Kentucky hills. With these latter types of alcohol manufacturing, quart and pint and occasionally, gallon jars seal and hold the clear liquid by product of Kentucky corn growers anonymous. It was these containers I saw under the hay in the loft of the barn as I helped Willie look for eggs laid in nests made by rogue chickens.

It was near seven o'clock and one of the Marion girls had cut a large watermelon lengthwise and placed both halves on the edge of the porch. She asked if I would like to have a slice of melon and a coke. I took both. Celebrating Independence Day with our neighbors was a lot of fun. They were patriotic and each hour brought more singing and dancing from the family. Everybody's performance was in a different key with some members choosing a key of their own invention. More of them began to join in the ceremony. I thought it strange to see men who normally exhibited quiet and shy behavior begin to sing to the tops of their voices and kick their bare feet higher than their overall straps. Burl began to swing Mae around and around while Earsel danced with a broom. I heard the same Yahoooing and Whoooping I had heard that morning the boys decided to take a ride on the mules. I laughed so much my teeth hurt and I was beside myself with joy until the two older boys began discharging shotguns into the air. It was then that all the family pets began finding a new hiding place. The ka-booming sounds seemed to have heightened the effect of alcohol and the releasing of stress. They were a stress-free family now.

When dusk began to settle over the valley, I knew that I needed to go home. Because darkness was soon to be everywhere, I decided to take the dirt road home. This way was farther, but safer than the path through the dark woods. Halfway down the hill, I lost my watermelon and coke. My head began to hurt and then it felt like it might burst . Again and again I lost more watermelon and coke. I reasoned that I could not have eaten that much melon and I drank only one coke.

Set Another Place at the Table

My eyes began to tear up so much I couldn't see the road ahead of me. My chest hurt from the hurling. I was so glad to make it home and hoped nobody in my family offered any watermelon.

That night my dad, mom, my sister and brothers quietly sat on the porch for a long time listening to the third world war being fought at the Marion's place. There would have been no need to try to sleep for a while or until those shy Marion boys ran out of fireworks. In my mind, I could still see them dancing.

Cursing Contest

Louie was a preacher's son and he and his family came home with us after church. This happened a lot as I grew up and I became acquainted with many preachers' children. After we ate a late lunch, we went outside to explore as young boys are supposed to do. I thought it would be a neat thing to do if we walked up to Willie's house and played with him and his brothers. Louie agreed and we took the short cut through the woods which came out into a clearing below the house. I was the fearless leader and felt at home on my own turf. I was being a knowledgeable guide and I was pointing at this tree and showing this rock and making up things as I went along. Then, my tour was interrupted when pandemonium broke loose inside the House of Marion. Cursing, shouting, yelling and screaming started coming from their house and the stir stopped me in my tracks. Moreover, I had my friend Louie, a preacher's son with me and he was hearing all these verbal assaults coming from my other friend Willie's house. I was so embarrassed. I thought about grabbing Louie and placing my hands over his ears. Surprisingly, Louie was grinning from ear to ear. He started laughing out loud. He started cheering them on! I didn't understand. He was a preacher's son.

Willie soon came outside and saw us standing on his porch.

Set Another Place at the Table

He didn't apologize for anything. He didn't seem to notice my ears that had turned bright red when I heard all the cursing. I introduced Louie to Willie and asked him if he wanted to do something. It made me feel better when he said yes and suggested we go to the barn and swing on the rope. We took turns swinging while another boy pushed. Things went along fine until Louie accidentally bumped against the barn door on his return trip on the rope swing. Then, I went into a shock-related trance and denied that I had heard Louie, the preacher's son let out an oath that would create a storm strong enough to sink a battleship.

Not to be outdone, Willie went one better and said one of those %$%$#%^!'s. Louie countered with (**)&$(&,T! And then the contest was on. The two combatants were toe to toe slinging verbal assaults that rivaled the fireworks over Fort Sumter. Louie was a preacher's son. I felt like applauding. I was still shaking my head in disbelief when we reached my house. My vocabulary was increasing and we weren't in school.

Uncle Raymond Comes to Visit

The man wore a suit coat and a white shirt with a necktie that had been loosened and turned away from center. His black pants reached down to partially cover black shoes that leaned over to the outside. He was a lean, tall man who wore his hat tilted backward enough to show a long forehead and long strands of hair that stuck out from under the brim. He was carrying two brown suitcases which he sat down every time he took ten steps or so. When he reached the square rock step at the front of Marvin's wooden porch, he stopped. He took a dirty handkerchief from his coat pocket and wiped his face and replaced the cloth. He sounded exhausted as he asked Marvin and me how to get to the Marbury place. Both Marvin and I pointed toward the road that led up the hill to where the Marions lived.

"Couldn't hire you two young lads to help an old man carry these two pieces of cargo, could I? I'd be more that grateful to you. I've come a long way." We looked at each other and agreed we would help. It took both Marvin and me to carry one of the pieces of luggage. We whispered about the weight and tried to guess what was inside these weighty bags. We had never worked this hard for anyone before. Twenty minutes later, the suitcases were sitting on the Marion's porch and the man knocked at their door. Nobody stirred inside the house.

There's a fairy tale that relates a story about a family of bears who take a walk through the woods and a curious, blond-haired visitor comes around. She enters the house that belongs to the bears without permission and makes herself at home. My story would have had some similarities but a tired man waited for permission to enter this home. It would appear that the owners were not home but that theory was shot when someone inside the house sneezed and the "kazoom" was heard out on the porch. Finally, Burl came to the door and told us to come on in. I sensed the lack of enthusiasm in his voice. Uncle Raymond had come to visit a while.

I never learned Uncle Raymond's last name and whose uncle he claimed to be or how he knew the Marion family. Willie didn't volunteer this information and I didn't ask. The man was still there after several days. One day he and Burl rode down the hill in the big Dodge truck and was gone quite a while. It was nearly dark and Marvin and I were catching lightening bugs and keeping them in a glass jar. The headlights of the truck lit up the road as the two men returned with a big load of something covered with a tarp on the back of the truck. We could see the silhouette against the evening sky. The clinging and clanking of the contents under the tarpaulin continued as the truck climbed the hill and went out of sight.

Nearly every day, Burl drove his truck down the hill and he and Uncle Raymond would stay gone until dusk had settled in the valleys. During this time, I saw none of the Marion children so Marvin and I spent our time together doing things like walking down our hollow road to get the mail, walking to the farthest field to chase the cows home, and other fun activities. Almost daily, we would have to hike up the steep hill by his house and turn the pole that held the television antenna. The wind would sometimes turn it around enough to miss the signal and the picture would not be clear or would not come in on the set at all. At the site of the antenna, one was high enough on the hill so he could see far away in all directions. I had not noticed before but one could see the Marion's house and farm from there. The distance from our place on the hill to the other side was too great to see clearly but both Marvin and I saw a fire that burned near a cliff shelter located a few hundred yards from their house.

Tall trees covered the area around the rock but we could see the flame as it lit up a small space underneath the canopy. We were curious as to why the neighbors would be burning anything at this time of evening. It was in the month of June and gardens were already producing so seed beds wouldn't need to be burned and this flame that we saw was deep in the forest. When Marvin asked his dad about the flame, he told us that it was none of our business as long as our neighbors kept it up on their hill. We were still curious and determined to explore this area soon.

Some days later, I asked Marvin if he would like to take a walk through the woods to find the reason for the flame we had seen a few nights ago. He had lost interest and wouldn't

Set Another Place at the Table

go with me. The television was on and the Cartwrights were in trouble out on the Ponderosa so he wanted to stay and find out how they got out of this one. I was not in any hurry to go through the woods by myself so I stayed and watched the show with my friend and soon forgot about all else. He also was not in the mood to come to my house and help my brother and me split and stack firewood for mom's kitchen stove. My brothers and I were busy stacking wood in our shed to be used this winter when Willie and Robert and their two dogs came up the road. They stopped to watch us work.

The two brothers didn't pick up a stick of wood or offer to help but they kept us entertained by smoking, spitting and cursing. All three of these habits were some that the boys had mastered and my brothers and I marveled at how good they could do each of them. Somehow, while the boys were demonstrating these masterful feats, our conversation turned to Uncle Raymond. Between piercing oaths that ionized the atmosphere around us and forming clouds of foul-smelling smoke from their self-rolled cigarettes, the two boys told us stories while we stacked the wood in piles to dry in the sun. They were willing to talk about him now and told us a great deal about this man. The boys told about many wars he had fought and whose side he had been on, how many fights he had won, how many countries around the world he had seen and how many presidents he had helped elect. The two boys seemed proud that their uncle had done and seen so much and that he had returned from his travels to allow some time

for the only family he had left. Uncle Raymond had even let Burl help him in a new financial interest he wanted to start right there on their farm. Now he and their father worked together and in a few weeks, things would be hunky-dory.

The Marions had planted some extra corn in the field near the cemetery and watched with anticipation as the plants matured and ears formed on each stalk. These corn plants had received much attention from Burl and Raymond as they fertilized and watered and weeded. Their work had produced a crop worthy to grace the front page of "American Corn Farmer" magazine. Uncle Raymond was too old to fight any more wars or travel across the world in search of a country needing a mercenary but he still had enough energy to grow corn and turn that resource into a valuable asset. Corn in another form was transported down Marbury hill at night while other friends of Uncle Raymond waited to complete this transaction by taking all his product.

The fire continued to burn at night near the rock cliff down under the tall trees. Burl and his partner made weekly trips down the hill and out the hollow. They stayed gone a long while each time. The tarp covered the load on the flatbed truck. The truck returned in the wee hours of the morning.

Uncle Raymond bought new dresses for Sue, Iris and Rosy. Robert, Willie and Earsel had new overalls and caps that had patches embroidered on the fronts above the visor. Burl bought new tires for the front of his red truck and Mae bought new shoes for herself and Josiah. The two older boys bought pistols and ammunition.

One night the roar of the red Dodge could be heard coming down the hill and producing a sound much like a machine gun blaattin-blaatting. A large black tarp covered a full load that appeared ghostly as it silhouetted against the night-time sky. The truck stayed gone a long while and when it returned, lighted cigarettes moved through the darkness of the cab like fireflies in a glass jar. The flatbed was bare once more and the engine seemed much less strained as it pulled the hill and came to rest in front of the Marion house.

As Burl and his partner were sleeping late the next day, two men in a car with an official license tag drove up to

Set Another Place at the Table

Marvin's house. The two gentlemen were dressed in blue suits with ties and blue pants that reached down to meet polished black boots. They both wore shaded glasses. They walked up to the square rock that was used for a step for the porch and asked for information on how to get to the Marion place. Marvin pointed to the dirt road that led up the hill. The men turned the car around and headed there.

Uncle Raymond and his two suitcases took up most of the back seat as the official car came back down the hill and drove on out the hollow. Now-a-days, the fire doesn't burn anymore underneath the tall trees next to the rock cliff near the Marion farm. Often, I can hear the two older two boys shoot for practice with their own pistols. Willie, Earsel and Robert wear their hats with embroidered patches and the overalls that their uncle bought for them. The new tires look good on the big, red Dodge truck and Mae doesn't hurt her feet as much when she wears her new shoes. Burl doesn't plan to grow as much corn next year. They don't expect Uncle Raymond to be back very soon.

Josiah Marion

Josiah Marion began his travels through this life with many disadvantages. He lacked enough oxygen during birth and waited far too long for his first gulp of air. His spindly legs refused to carry his small body for long walks. He spent much of his time on the couch or on the floor so he could crawl or sometimes walk to the next room. His language didn't develop with his age so his communication skills were severely lacking. As a result of his lack of ability to make progress in these areas, Burl and Mae kept him home from school and realized this was the best they could provide for their afflicted child.

Josiah's eyes were bright, at times. They shone with delight when a brother or sister would hold him up in the air and maybe let go momentarily only to catch him again. The siblings were sure he giggled each time though he made no sound. He was carried to and from everywhere. It was understood that somebody had to "tote" little brother and that responsibility was willingly shared by all. The two older brothers made a fuss over Josiah when they would walk through the room. Willie, Robert or Earsel had him up on the saddle when they rode the pony. The girls decorated his little face with their makeup almost like he was their baby doll. Mae held him in her lap when they sat to eat meals. She spooned the food to his mouth and cleaned his face when the food was smeared up to his ears. But the small one was not expected to grow older with the others.

Burl and Mae worked all year for twenty seven hundred dollars. Maybe there were a few dollars made here and there by picking up aluminum cans for recycling or selling garden crops to neighbors and even depending upon nature for providing ginseng or yellow root herbs to sell for cash. This amount was all there was and Josiah needed more medicine. The Marion family needed help. Some help was on the way.

The physical education teacher at Brickyard elementary school was a good man. He was tough and strict and his attitude was downright mean at times. He was a good man, however. He came to my classroom one day and asked that I come with him to his office. Mr. Bob assured me that I was in no trouble but that he wanted to ask some questions about Josiah Marion. I told him what I knew. He thanked me and said I could return to class.

Brickyard Elementary once hosted high school basketball games in the full-sized gymnasium. Grades one through twelve attended classes in better times. On this night in October, there was little room for moving without bumping into someone. The place was full of kind country folk and concerned city families. People from nearby counties came to be part of the benefit to raise money for little Josiah Marion so his medicine could be bought. Burl stood outside the gym and smoked another rolled cigarette while he tucked his shirt tail into his pants. The Marion children had worn their best clothes and my mom had seen that their hair had been washed and combed. Then, Mr. Brach started talking into the microphone. All was quiet in the packed gym.

An auction, a pie supper, a dance, cake walks and a sack race were a few of the events taking place that evening. These fun things and many more helped raise nearly a thousand dollars that night toward buying what Josiah needed. Burl and Mae were in tears as they held Josiah up in their arms and thanked everyone for coming and helping. All the Marion children behaved admirably.

Josiah's health failed considerably despite the efforts made by doctors and the medicine helped for only a short while. With the family having no health insurance, needed medical care of this extent was not to be acquired. Shortly before Thanksgiving that year, Earsel knocked on our door and told my dad what had happened. Dad drove Earsel down to a neighbor's house and used their phone to call the authorities. Josiah passed on and was buried in a nearby county cemetery.

I had not witnessed a death in the family before and didn't know how to react to the news and found that Willie and his brothers didn't know how either. I kept quiet during the wake and stayed outside most of the time. It was the custom to keep the deceased for a couple of days and allow family time for viewing and grieving. It seemed so weird to have someone die and then keep him here in the living room. Our family went to visit the Marion's house that next night. We stayed only a little while and I was very near to shedding tears when my mother told me it was time to go home. That was okay with me.

Strawberry Patch

From the window of the school bus, I could see the carefully cultivated rows of strawberries in full bloom. It was the latter days of the month of May and this meant that the first berries would be turning red in a short while. The Street family owned the farm that ran alongside the highway and the patch of fruit could be seen while traveling east on this road. Mr. Street taught at the university and farming was his first love. He and his wife hired my brothers and me to work on the farm. This offered us the opportunity to make a little spending money during the year. It was the job of picking strawberries that I remember the most.

At other times, my brothers and I might cut the grass, pick weeds from the growing plants in the garden or grub roots from the ground so they wouldn't grow back. Mr. Street subscribed to many of the popular magazines dealing with the newest techniques in farming. He would read them from cover to cover and use this information with his own growing crops. He was highly successful when turning his shallow soils to fertile loams. He supplemented his income by selling fruits and vegetables to folks in town. It was his strawberry crop, however, that demanded most of his attention and much of ours.

Set Another Place at the Table

With several children in the neighborhood who needed to make extra money, a labor force was ready made. Each young man or woman would be assigned an area to pick the berries. A picker would stand, sit, squat or scoot down the area between two rows of strawberry plants. This area is called a "balk". From this point, one could reach left and right to pick the fruit from both sides. The ripe berries would be placed in wooden quart baskets. When the basket was filled, it was placed in a wooden carrier which looked much like a hand-made tool box. Six baskets filled with strawberries could be carried safely in one of these containers. For each of these baskets filled with ripe strawberries, we would receive five cents. Usually, I could pick twenty baskets per day.

When the Marion kids chose to come and pick, Mr. and Mrs. Street became anxious. The neighbor children didn't possess the work ethic necessary to pick strawberries for any length of time. When the sun rose higher in the sky and the temperature rose accordingly, the Marion kids lost their will to work any more. They found it more interesting to irritate another person who worked a few rows across the patch. Often an unsuspecting picker received a strawberry missle by air when it landed on his back, head, or face. One of the Marion kids would find a large, overripe berry and throw it across the field and strike another worker. The red stain from the smashing strawberry would show on someone's shirt or dress. Some kids would go tell Mr. or Mrs. Street while others would retaliate by throwing another berry back at him. Then, the fight was on. The warriors would step on the plants, spill baskets of strawberries and keep the other workers from picking any more. The Streets were usually kind, but would ask those guys to leave.

Mr. Street owned a green, fifty one Chevrolet car. At the end of the day of picking, he would load the baskets into this car and head to town. Here, he would peddle his fruit to his teaching friends and make some money. Along with the ripe strawberries, he would sell grapes, black berries, asparagus and other vegetables. He was a careful salesman and took exact notes. He and his wife made sure that a check for ten percent of this income was given to the Methodist Church which they attended.

At Christmas time, the couple would make a visit to our house and deliver some gifts. We never expected much but the thought of giving was well received by our family. One of the gifts I received many times was a pair of Jersey gloves with a coin inserted into each finger of the glove. It may be a nickle or a dime. Other gifts we got were made of cloth that were sewn by Mrs. Street. From our house, the wonderful neighbors went up the hill to the Marion's house. All the children received a gift from the Street family.

The owners of the strawberry farm were never critical of anybody. Although many times they became irritated with the behavior of the Marion kids, they forgave and hired them back to pick more berries. They saw the good in everyone and helped with any thing their friends need them to do. The Streets were older citizens but continued to work on their farm for many years. Finally, Mrs. Street passed away and Mr. Street lost his house to a fire. He had much difficulty with reasoning skills after that catastrophe. Today, some grand children live on the farm but no strawberries are grown there.

Cash Crop

Certain responsibilities within the Marion family were assigned and remarkably, these jobs were done without question. They were the year-long chores associated with the raising of burley tobacco. The family members worked toward that day in late November or early December when the hard work of raising and preparing the tobacco was finished. A check was presented by the buyers down at the warehouse in town. One half of the money was owed to the landowner and the rest was small pay for the fruits of their labors. Usually, the check was presented a few weeks before Christmas and all nine children could have some nice gift to open on that morning.

The cash crop was the main source of money for the year and the importance of trying to raise a crop as good or better than last year was the goal. With the entire family old enough and strong enough to work in the tobacco fields, short work was made of the task of keeping the rows free of weeds. The same was true of ridding the plants of a large worm that could destroy the crop within days. Thus a constant watch was kept for the first infestation of these leaf-eating catapillars. For eight years, the tobacco was in good hands.

Not only did the Marion family raise tobacco, they used

the product. All the children but Robert smoked cigarettes or cigars. The men chewed and spit, constantly. I never saw any of the girls chew tobacco, but I didn't go in their house very often. After lunch, they smoked. While working outside, they smoked. While taking a break, while plowing, while cutting wood and before they went to bed, they lit up a cigarette. A cigarette machine which rolled loosely ground tobacco leaves sat on the table in the kitchen. I have watched Willie roll twenty cigarettes while talking to me about something. The little red roller took loose tobacco leaf, a cigarette paper and pronto! A handsome white cigarette rolled out and looked as if it said "smoke me, I'm ready".

The Marion kids were talented to think of ways to entertain themselves. Since they had very little money, they stayed at home and worked and played. When no tobacco was hanging in the barn hallway, a plow rope could be attached to the top tier pole in the barn and make a swing. In the wide hallway, one could fly up, up and away with the greatest of ease. Rosy was scared to be pushed very high because she couldn't see very well and Blythe was rather small for his age but Earsel, Robert and Willie were very impressive when they swung through the hallway and briefly through the wide open front door and return to slide to a halt on the dirt floor. Robert was pretending to be a circus trapeze artist when the ashes of his cigarette dropped from his lip and burned his bare chest. He was at the zenith of his pendulum swing when he let go of the rope to catch his smoking cigarette.

Set Another Place at the Table

Robert's arm looked like the eighteenth letter of the alphabet as we tied it loosely to two broken tobacco sticks and made a makeshift splint. With tears rolling from his eyes, he tried to raise his splinted arm to wave goodbye to us from the back of the big red Dodge flatbed truck.

Rosy was scared to walk from the barn to the house because she couldn't see very well. I accompanied her. The rope was taken down because it was needed for guiding the mule when the tobacco fields needed plowing again.

Marbury Hill

The county fiscal court took care of roads leading to the many cemeteries around the area but limited their services to coincide with a burial at that site. Sometimes, a long time elapsed before some family chose to bring their loved one back to our county and Marbury cemetery for their final resting place. In the meantime, heavy rains and snow eroded the dirt surface to expose the rocks and clay that made up the road bed. These conditions made it difficult for automobiles to travel over this rough surface to visit either the Marion house or the graveyard. There were some negotiations that took place between land owners and the district magistrate who may be holding office at that time. The politics of how to spend county tax dollars created a game of strategy for each four-year term in office. To assure reelection to an office for another term, political promises were made in return for the votes of an entire family. The Marion votes would count in the next election. Five of the members of this family were registered to cast their ballot in the November election.

In the early nineteen sixties, wooden bridges spanned the many streams that traversed through the valleys and the task of keeping new timbers on each structure cost the county a lot of money. Our road alone had three of these low-water wooden spans. As they deteriorated with each year that passed, the amount of weight that could safely travel across would be limited even more. Soon, the bridges would have to be replaced. We were soon to boast of three new wooden structures and a freshly-graveled road on which to travel.

At our house, many men and women who were seeking office came to ask for our support and to vote for them when we went to the polling place. They left books of matches, cards, fingernail files, flags and paper fans with wooden handles. These items were colorful and bore their name and the office sought after on each. After a short visit, they politely left without receiving any positive response from my dad. He never discussed the freedoms of politics or bank accounts with anyone. They had better luck with the Marions, however.

Seasoned politicians stayed a while with our neighbors when they made their visits. These present or past office holders knew they would have to give more of themselves to a family who had bargaining power. Five votes could be had if negotiations worked out. Money worked, and so did whiskey. A trip out to the trunk of the automobile driven by the office seeker yielded a bottle or two of wine or whiskey and maybe a six pack of beer. Burl bargained for his bevy of votes and in return for his promise, collected handsomely for his efforts.

The first week in November was an anxious time for the voters in this area. Based on the outcome of the election, many would have a good four years or a term without many perks.

Set Another Place at the Table

School board members, county judge, magistrates, sheriff, county attorney and others filed for office and ran campaigns for months before the day of the election. A well-run campaign left nothing unchecked on the list of things to do. No household was left unvisited. No baby went without being held or bragged about and sometimes even kissed by a politician. Tuesday morning, however brought finality to many people's dreams. Somebody would win, many would not.

A big, red Dodge truck with a flat bed rolled up to the voting house driveway. It was met by several card pushers and persons who used these last minutes trying to persuade those few who had not decided to cast their vote for a particular candidate. Burl, Mae, Roy, Troy and Earsel walked in a straight row looking neither to the left nor to the right and approached the voting house door looking confident. Robert and Willie sat on the back of the flatbed and rolled themselves a cigarette and smoked. The two boys showed no emotion and paid more attention to the ash on the end of their cigarettes than to what was going on around them. Burl and his family of voters soon returned from the voting house. The truck wore no bumper stickers nor did it have any candidate's name on the windshield. There were no political party flags flying on the aerial wire. No indication of how the five voters cast their ballots could be guessed. It was too early for them so show any loyalty and would wait until a winner was announced. Only then would it be safe to declare loyalty to whichever candidate won the elections.

Set Another Place at the Table

Late that election night, the Marions listened intently as the election results were given over the radio. Whether a favorite candidate won another term in office or a new candidate won for the first time, the neighbors paid attention and shifted their loyalty to either direction. It didn't matter which side of the fence they were on, the Marions could jump, ride or straddle. Seldom did they fall off.

There is an art to the chore of asking for favors from an elected official. Some people do it well. One way is to approach the official with hat in hand and show a helpless side and seemingly ask for pity and compassion. Another way is to boldly go forward and use political clout and voter pressure to convince the office holder of your weight in the arena. My friends knew how to use both methods but used them only after the official had been studied and labeled. They asked other people who had success with coming before the judge or magistrate or sheriff to ask for something. They learned what had worked and had checked the voting record of this individual. They knew how many times he or she had said no or yes. When all the homework had been done, they moved. The Marions wanted two loads of coal to be hauled to their house so they could burn it to help heat their house that winter. This newly-elected judge had established a reputation very early in his short career of being a "No" man.

Burl chose to approach this request with method number one and ask for this favor person to person. He took Mae and Rosy with him. Rosy "toted" Josiah in her arms. Josiah was not toilet trained and carried this morning's movement with him. Taking his hat from his head, Mr. Marion spoke softly to the judge about the coming winter and how much this coal would be needed for winter's fuel. He watched the judge's face to ascertain any clue about which way he might be leaning. Rosy stepped closer while holding baby Josiah in her arms. Mae stepped closer and lit a cigarette and began puffing. She offered the lit cigarette to Burl who puffed, took a deep draw and exhaled toward the judge. While turning different shades of color, the judge wiped sweat from his brow and agreed that two loads of coal should be taken to the Marion residence on Marbury hill. Burl thanked His Honor, shook his hand and started to leave. As the family started to leave, the judge stood up and said, "Tell your daughter she has a pretty baby. Go, now and take care of it."

Tobacco Stripping Language Lesson

Profanity was a way of life and a common way of communication within the Marion family. Children learned expletives before they developed teeth. Each word was learned by listening to brothers, sisters or parents who modeled the art of cursing for the younger ones. This display of another side of the English language was foreign to me because we never used it in or around our house. I couldn't develop the zing and zin to pull off some of the oaths that were so eloquently spoken by our new neighbors. It seemed so natural for them and the most common of requests from Burl or Mae took on a new zeal when these strong and spicy words were attached to the requests. November was tobacco stripping time and it was inside the makeshift stripping room where I was introduced to a new area of farming cash crops while learning a whole new language.

Burley tobacco leaves require several weeks to dry before it can be stripped of its leaves and it is these leaves that are taken to market to be sold. After the tobacco is cut and transported from the fields to be hung in the barn for a while, the leaves dry and turn different shades of brown. Then, one cool day in the month of November, conditions become right for taking the leaves from the stalks by hand. This condition with just the right amount of moisture still left inside the leaves is known as being in "case." Farmers feel their tobacco to determine if conditions are right for removing the leaves. This procedure is called tobacco stripping. Leaves are collected in bunches where the stems are pointed in the same direction. Each fist full is called a "hand". A large fist full of one kind or color of leaves is wrapped and tied tightly around the stems by another folded leaf. Several of these hands are packed tightly and shipped off to market and sold.

To control temperature and moisture in the tobacco barn, a temporary room is constructed somewhere within the barn. Stalks of tobacco are carried into this room to be stripped. Three or four people handle the tobacco and each take certain leaves for their hand. Choosing which leaf to pull is an art which is learned at an early age. With a family with as many children as the Marions, two crews can work together and double the speed at which the tobacco crop is finished.

I wanted to watch this activity and be of assistance so one day I ventured into the barn while this project was being worked on. Willie said I could help if I wanted to carry stalks out of the room and take them away to a place out behind the barn. At this very time, my friend, my playmate and my classmate repeated the very words he had said that one day in the classroom when he refused to give his book report orally. It was not having to deliver a book report today that prompted his cursing. It was a sharp splinter on a dry stalk of tobacco that pierced his finger on his right hand. It didn't bleed much.

Set Another Place at the Table

I later thought that the cursing stopped the bleeding. My ears turned bight red anyway from the shock.

From all over the barn, expletives came flying! From the loft where Earsel was lifting some tobacco down to Robert an oath exploded with such force it achieved some personality as it flew past my ears. Rosey cursed when she turned too sharply and ran into the open barn door. Rosey was almost blind and didn't know it. Blythe gave an award-winning rendition of what to do with a hand of tobacco that Sue had asked him to put into the tobacco press. Iris wanted to go to the house to warm up but was denied permission by her father, Burl. The conversation that ensued between Iris and Burl would convince a sailor to jump ship at the next port. Not only were there ****'s but several *&*&*#&'s and a whole bunch of #%%#!!'s and an occasional riveting ^%$&**&^%!!. I don't think bleeps would mask out these barrages. When I walked home later, my mom asked me where I'd been and what I had been doing. I was literally at a loss for words when I tried to explain to mom. I know she questioned the look of bewilderment and disbelief I wore on my face that afternoon. It was really enough to make me want to applaud.

The Halloween Mules

Halloween night used to be a dangerous time for children to be out and about. It was the one night of the year a youngster could behave deviously and get away with it. It grew to be a night of revenge for deeds done earlier in the year. For instance, Trick or Treat holiday became an excuse for Trick to be independent of Treat. I always wondered where young adolescents learned that setting a bag of cow manure on fire on an old person's porch was funny. The owner of the house panicked when he or she saw the burning bag and attempted to extinguish the flames by stomping on the mess. Or when did the misdeed of pushing an outhouse over get started? Needless to say my neighbors, the Marions knew these tricks and a lot more.

The moon didn't shine on Halloween night that year at my house. It didn't rain, but was threatening to start at any moment. I don't remember just how I was allowed to be with the three left-handed Marion boys, but I was. Neither Mom or Dad would be proud of me if they knew what a terribly funny thing I took part in. Nobody got hurt and no property was destroyed but I just don't think my parents would have seen the humor as I did.

Earsel could strike a match with his left hand only. I don't know if Willie or Robert could so their older brother was the official designated match striker for the night. We didn't go to our neighbor's houses and ask for candy like the smaller kids. We headed for "Jake's Field" to have some fun with the mules. Willie hadn't forgiven the mule for sending him over the fence that morning while walking to school. I had learned a little about mules from the boys while watching them plow or use the work animals to drag poles from the woods to be cut up for firewood. It was while watching this type of work that I soon learned that walking behind a mule was a task for which one dealt with a lot of gas being produced by the animals. It seemed that for every pass the team made, they passed gas. Sometimes I think the animals were having fun with the boys and in their own way shared the joke. I wish I could know what they were thinking. The Marion boys knew when to anticipate these extrusions and ducked or walked out of the way of the smell. I hadn't learned that much yet.

In the darkness of this Halloween night, Earsel and Robert climbed the barbed wire fence and quietly walked up to the shadows of Jake's two mules. It wasn't very long until I heard Robert whisper, "Now!, light the mule!". It was glorious! Halloween night lit up like a meteor as a lighted mule ran blindly across the horizon. My sides hurt yet when I remember Halloween, nineteen sixty.

No animals were hurt during Halloween night, nineteen sixty, by four trick-r-treaters who found humor in the antics that farm boys perform.

The Broken Gun

Squirrel season opens around the middle to the last week in August. This important date draws many weekend marksmen to Kentucky to show their expertise in shooting small-gauge shotguns in quest of the gray or red squirrel. The tops of the hills along wooded ridges are the best places to find the game. The illusive tree climbers are actively searching for nuts for eating and storage. When the animals are chewing on the thick hulls of the hickory nut, walnut or the beech nut, pieces of the nut and the hull drop to the bottom of the forest floor. Hunters say the squirrels are "cutting" on a particular food at that time. These signs are easily spotted and give the hunter a clue as to where the activity is going on.

Elmo's older son seem to be roaming through the woods more than half his waking hours. He knew the forest like the back of his hand and developed into a very good hunter. He especially liked to shoot squirrels. He brought them home and prepared them for skillet frying and the family ate each and every one he bagged.

Sometimes the hunt can become frustrating when the day doesn't go as planned. For instance, briars can tear at your pants and shoes while walking through the forest. Insects can pester your ears and eyes at the moment you need to be the quietest. The squirrel can hide from you by holding closely to the trunk of the tree or lie flatly while out on the limb. You can't shoot what you can't see. What if the frustration you experience is with a faulty gun?

I remember a twenty-gauge shotgun that belonged to the Marion family and was used by one of the older boys when he hunted. With this gun, one could be assured that the weapon would fall apart when fired. Even with black electrical tape wrapped around the forearm and stock, the gun fell apart each time it was discharged. A second rapid shot was out of the question because the gun had to be put back together before it was fired again.

This hunter practiced the art of repairing the old gun much like a quick-draw artist would work to gain speed with his gun. He would fire, put the gun back together quickly, load and fire again in just seconds. Because of the time spent in the woods and the practice with this old shotgun, this Marion older son did a lot to destroy the ecological balance by shooting far too many animals in the food chain. At least two years passed before there were squirrels roaming through the hickories.

Blackberry Wine

During the first two weeks of July, Kentucky produces large quantities of blackberries from uncultivated vines. The fruit matures at this time and the season for picking lasts only two weeks or so. This delicacy can be used for eating, canning, baking, topping for ice cream or pudding, or to produce a fermented version of home-made wine. The art of fermentation and wine making usually requires a climate-controlled factory and a few generations of family secrets thrown in the mix. In the case of the Marion family, all that was required was a large crock pot called a buttermilk churn, some cane sugar and some starting malt. These ingredients can be bought at the local food store. With a gallon or so of fermenting blackberries, nature's chemistry starts to act and the resulting product is an alcohol-based concoction that either stands one up to attention or knocks one to the floor.

The stronger of the two mixtures is the goal toward which one strives.

School was out and it was the summer between seventh and eighth grades. Willie and I saw an opportunity to make some spending money if we sold blackberries. The fruit brought decent prices and we picked several gallons. My friend had stated earlier in the week that his brothers wanted two gallons for their own use. Again, I was naïve to think that two young men could eat that many berries. However, I was polite and didn't question their purpose. It was later next week that I began to understand what they were doing with all that fruit.

Nature's own way of dealing with plants that contain sugar is a mystery. Scientists, farmers, and housewives have used these naturally-occurring chemical reactions for ages and in many helpful ways. The process of fermentation turns the liquid part of this reaction into some form of alcohol and the Marions found that blackberry wine cures many of the ills that confound people. The two gallons of ripe blackberries that were given to the Marion brothers were poured into a five-gallon churn and mixed with yeast and sugar. The container was covered and left to"work" for a few days. From time to time, Willie and I became curious and raised the lid to check on the progress. We left the barn with fascination for the smell coming from the old churn. The Marion boys left the barn light headed and a fascination for the brew.

Gone Fishing

Kentucky ranks second in fresh-water streams in the nation. The state of Alaska holds the distinction of being first. Alaskan streams freeze over many months of the year, however, and we didn't live in Alaska anyway but possessing information like this makes one feel good. Many of these creeks and waterways in our commonwealth abound with aquatic life and most any "water hole" will produce some types of fish. As soon as water temperatures in the streams rose to levels above forty degrees, our neighbors started wading the creeks in search of just about any size minnow, crawdad, tadpole or salamander that could be used for fish bait. Two main methods of catching these aquatic animals were used. One way was called "noodling".

Chest deep in the cold water, one or more of the boys would use his hands to feel under a rock or a tree root and slowly run his fingers alongside whatever fish that may be lurking under there. More likely than not, a silver-sided fish would be brought to the surface while it flipped and tried to slip loose from a hand that was reddened from the cold water. Fish that were lucky not to get caught by the method above were sure to fall prey to seineing. Seineing consisted of slowly dragging one of Burl's cotton tobacco-bed coverings along the bottom of the creek bed. One arm appeared just under the surface of the water and held the top and the other arm held the cloth along the bottom while walking upstream. Raising the cloth up from time to time produced several flipping crawdads, many shiny minnows and an occasional water snake.

If farming chores were done on Friday evening, Burl took the entire family to the river for a weekend of fishing and camping. Again, the big red Dodge truck would head down the hill with engine backfiring and sounding like a firing squad. With enough fish bait caught and kept in kegs of cool water, the Marions were prepared to stay on the creek bank as long as necessary. With a collection of cane poles and fishing line, bleach bottles and firewood, they were off to try to make a dent in the catfish population.

I was asked to accompany the family on one of these expeditions but mom just shook her head when I asked permission. She never offered an explanation as to why she preferred that I not go along. I always thought she was worried that I might not come back. It's true I couldn't swim very well.

On Sunday afternoon, we could hear the truck roaring up our hollow on the return trip.

On a couple of occasions, I waited by the road until the truck came so I could see what types and how many fish they had caught from the river. I would know many of the species but some I could not recognize. Catfish seemed the fish to be caught most often but I saw several suckers and some that I later learned later were carp. The boy's faces and shoulders were bright red from sunburning and they lay across the bed of the truck looking exhausted from the weekend of fishing. The girls rode up front in the truck's cab but I could see sunburned arms and it didn't look like the redness stopped at the sleeves of their dresses. Nobody seemed too interested in anything on these Sunday evenings.

The Marions were worn out.

A New Batch of Puppies

Inevitably, families who fail to neuter or spay their pets find that nature has taken its course and new pets are on their way. I found this to be true with Janie and Turk, two female dogs that belonged to the neighbors. I guess I just didn't know what to look for when the dogs became pregnant so I paid them no mind when their bellies began dragging the ground. One day after school was over, Willie came to me and said he had a secret and that I could have three guesses as to what his secret was. I had no idea about his secret but he ended up telling me long before I had time to think about a guess. He didn't wait to give me any clues. His soft little secrets were hidden in a dug-out hole on top of the hill that stood above the cemetery. Their mommy could find them here and provide milk for their thirst. We walked there from school before going home.

The puppy with the softest nose took a liking to me and as days went by, the attachment became mutual. She was about the cutest thing I had ever seen. Willie gave her to me and said I could take her as soon as her mother weaned her. I thought about her quite a bit and made plans for her new home with me. My dog, Scotia, was older and was always tracking some animal and didn't hold still long enough to pet and cuddle.

I persuaded myself that it was time to have another dog at my house. I had not told my mother about this new idea. It was late in the evening when I brought the subject up before mom. Mom had a way of being absolute with her answers. I didn't get to bring the dog home.

Working Dogs

All the Marion children knew how to plow, harness a mule and plant seeds. They could place a harness on any four-footed animal in the barnyard. Willie and Robert hitched both their dogs, Janie and Turk side to side and used the dogs much like one would a mule team or a pair of horses. As long as the dogs were working together, they formed a team and actually pulled whatever load to which they would be hitched. If they were made to work individually, they sat down and no amount of coaxing would convince them to work at the task. The leather belts around their chests were cute and efficient. They looked much like tiny reindeer ready to work for Santa Claus.

The two boys asked if I could help them build a fort made of poles. The dogs would pull those trees to the site of our future outpost if I would cut the saplings down. "The best laid plans of dogs and men" sometimes go awry. It didn't take much time for the blisters, sweat and tiredness to overcome any need I had for a command post on the outskirts of my dad's land. Daniel Boone may have had the stamina but I didn't. Neither did the dogs. After I had cut only three poles, Earsel decided to have the dogs pull them to the site. The poor dogs tugged and panted until we untied one pole and had them try to pull only two. This worked much better and the dogs zipped right along until they came to the stream which flowed between our properties. There the dogs sat down in the cool water and stayed. We played something else less strenuous.

Yellow Jacket's Nest

Willie, Earsel and I knew that a yellow jacket's nest had been built directly in the path that led to a cliff shelter which was our favorite playground. We stepped wide and left them alone. We would come back at night and burn them out. This was done by pouring a little oil or kerosene directly down the entrance hole and striking a match to the fuel. As the inhabitants flew out to see what was going on with their home, the fire burned their wings. We made plans to do that deed tonight after dark when we knew all the insects were at home. We gave it no other thought because we were busy pretending to be either an Indian or cowboy.

This game was pretty simple. Cowboys defended the fort which the top of the big rock was designated and the marauding savages tried to enter the "fort" any way they could without getting shoved back off the rock. Since there were only three of us playing the game, we tired quickly and sat down to talk and eat sandwiches we brought. Rosy was heard faintly calling our names. She was coming to find us. Rosy was partially blind and would soon have glasses.

Rosy called our names which we recognized but all else she was yelling was not understandable. Then, screams mixed with expletives came at a steady but fierce rate. The yellow jackets had found her and were stinging her anywhere they found skin. We ran to help and found her on the ground screaming and rolling back and forth. We started slapping any insects left to slap and finally got them all. Poor Rosy was in such pain. So were we all. When we got to the Marion's house, we drew water from the well til our arms ached. Mae poured cool water over Rosy as she sat in a big metal tub the family used for canning beans. Her stings caused her face to swell to look much larger and made her look like a ripe strawberry. I felt really bad and wished I could do something. I walked and half ran to my house and asked mom what to do. She walked with me through the woods to take some ointment for the stings. She and Mae rubbed this medicine on Rosy from head to toe. I didn't tell her about the times I had gotten stung.

Chumley and the Fox Hunt

The Marbury cemetery was located high atop the hill past the house where the Marions stayed. A whitewashed fence separated the sacred place from the pasture field that surrounded it on all sides. The fiscal court was required to maintain the road that led up to the swinging gate that provided access to the burial sites. No more than twenty grave markers showed loved ones where kinfolk of older days had been laid for their final rest. The grass on the grounds were meticulously kept by the family whose name appeared on the wooden arch above the gate. Much like national cemeteries one visits on planned vacations around the country, The Marbury site was proudly kept but its size was much smaller.

Since the county government had ownership of the road leading to this burial site and a right-of-way on either side, anyone wanting to visit could legally do so. The Marions considered these visits an invasion of their privacy since the road ran within a few yards of their front porch. They built a crude gate using parallel pieces of barbed wire attached to a vertical post. The family would pull the barrier over and attach it to the upright post at the close of every day. The wire gate also doubled as a means to help keep some cattle from roaming down the county road and possibly walking away. This issue of blocking the county road made the docket of a fiscal court meeting.

The Marions came to supper again one evening and an

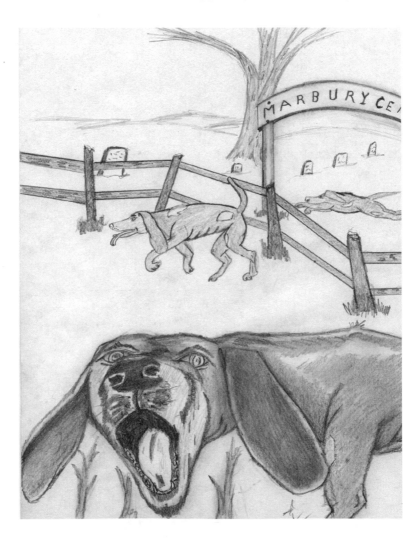

envelope showed from Burl's shirt pocket. I'm sure we had the usual food items ready for a family of five but Mom was prepared for more guests. After supper, my father read the letter to Mr. and Mrs. Marion and explained that the county officials have asked that the fence that blocked the road to the cemetery be removed this very day and then cóntinued to inform Mr. And Mrs. Marion as to the legality of the matter. Burl asked my dad what he would do in this case. Dad said that if he was in this trouble, he would take the fence down.

A man called Chumley lived a few miles away and was know for his large number of hunting dogs. He hunted squirrels, possum, quail, rabbits and rattlesnakes. He and his family ate the squirrels, possum, quail and rabbits. He made belts and hat bands with the skin of the rattlesnakes. He hunted alone most of the time. Most always, he set up all-night camping directly in front of the gate to Marbury Cemetery. His favorite type of this sport was fox hunting. At one time his neighbors complained that when all his twenty four fox hounds started barking, no one could hear what anyone was saying for miles around. He hunted alone because no one wanted to set their dogs loose when his hounds were on the trail. He and Burl clashed. The reasons were obvious.

The Marions defense at the court hearing consisted of complaining about the damage done by a large number of dogs while their owner was hunting on their property. Burl told the court judge that Chumley had driven his truck up the hill past their house and parked next to the cemetery gate.

Set Another Place at the Table

There he had loosed his dogs and the trouble began. The court did not rule because the hunter himself had not stepped foot on private property. The Marions were not happy. The feud that started between the Marions and Chumley never reached the press but was quite interesting. One must know about the sport of fox hunting to fully appreciate the feud.

Fox hunting is done at night in Kentucky. That is the time the grey or red fox creeps out from the underground den and looks for something to eat. They prefer chickens or field mice but will prey on many other smaller animals. No chicken is safe from these nocturnal four-footed predators. Fox hunting is a sport where the hunted never gets caught. The fox uses his cunning to elude the pack of dogs. The fox runs faster than the hounds and returns to escape through a back entrance to his den. The dogs learn to come back home when the hunter summoned them by blowing on an instrument made from a cow horn. The trumpeting sound could be heard for miles over those low Kentucky hills.

The thrill derived from this type of hunting is the chase. Lean, lanky, long-eared spotted hounds that have been bred primarily for this sport are loosed from their chains and the hunt begins. It's just a short time until their sensitive noses begin to sniff the grass, trees and bushes to pick up the scent left behind by a fox who has recently passed by.

The dog's owner memorizes the sound of the bark made by his dog. With so many of Chumley's dogs in the race, other owners could not hear the bark belonging to his own dogs.

Set Another Place at the Table

Arguments erupted around the campfire when one hunter claimed the bark of the lead dog was his own pure bred, "Happy". Another owner was sure that his dog, "Champion" was leading the hunt. Neither owner could be completely sure because of all the other dogs that Chumley entered into the race. Rules were made while standing around the campfires as to the number of dogs that could run at one time. Disagreements concerning this rule and others gave other competing fox hunters enough reasons to avoid hunting with Chumley.

Delirium abounds when the pack of hounds smells the strong scent of the fox and causes the dogs to pay no attention to boundary lines. Focusing on the chase, the long distance runners follow the fox anywhere it leads them. Farmers complain because gardens are sometimes destroyed by the running dogs. Patches of growing tobacco have been knocked down and trampled over and paths were made by the feet of the hounds while crashing through fields of clover. The Marions depended on the farm and the products they grew for their food supply and cash crops. Paybacks were coming and coming soon.

Chumley's old pickup truck was loaded with baying hounds as it passed by the Marion's house one Wednesday night. It had gotten dark and the entire family sat on the porch which surrounded the house on three sides. It's probably true that no friendly greeting was exchanged as the hunter chugged on up the hill toward the graveyard. He was not afraid to camp all night next to tombstones and had stated he was not afraid of anything, living or dead.

The dogs were loosed from their chains and they started the hunt. Chumley made a fire near the entrance to the cemetery. He prepared for the long night's hunt. However, there was no barking from the dogs, ever. No dogs returned, ever. Chumley waited all night for his fox hounds to come back to the truck so he could go home. Early the next morning, he tooted his horn to signal his dogs. Chumley hunted no more on the hill near the Marbury cemetery. Ever.

The Marions took the gate down and didn't block the county road again, ever.

Troy Goes Courting

The early dismissal bell rang at five minutes past three o'clock in the afternoon. This allowed time for the children who walked home to leave a little early and be well on their way before the buses came to transport the other pupils. Brickyard Elementary was astir with kids exiting their classrooms. Some rushed to the bathroom for a quick pit stop before hiking home while others chose to run out the door while still others sauntered around in no hurry whatsoever. I was more of a cautious middle-of-the-roader because I was in no hurry to get home but I didn't want to stay any longer in a place where seatwork was expected of all students. I lived with fear that one of my teachers would load me down with even more work just because they could. With books and weekend homework papers in hand, I started out the double entrance door which led onto the street in front of the school. The Marions usually came alongside to begin the after-school chatter at this time of the day but they were not to be seen until I got outside and onto the sidewalk that ran along the front of the building.

Burl had parked the big red Dodge truck directly in front of the classroom windows and was smoking a cigarette. Several of the Marion children were trying to get on board the flatbed while the girls were squeezing into the front seat. This scene reminded me of a movie I had watched on another neighbor's television about a sinking ship and all hands on deck were clamoring for a seat in the lifeboat. It was every man for him or herself. The truck was soon loaded. Willie's brother had a shirt on underneath his overalls!

It took me a while but I learned that one of the older Marion boy's name was Troy. His twin brother was Roy. I had never seen either young man wear a shirt. The two straps that held a pair of pants onto their lean bodies came up over their shoulders and fastened to a bib with pockets. Today Troy had a shirt on underneath and it was clean and it was white. Troy was going courting.

Tobacco cutting time in Kentucky is a timely event that must be done within a certain window. Harvest must wait until the chest-high plants have turned yellow but not brown. Each field of plants has its own maturity time. Tobacco farmers monitor this window and utilize manpower for this busy time of the year. Troy was very fast and efficient with a tobacco knife and a spear. He had been working for farmers in neighboring counties and his reputation had spread quickly. His efficiency and work ethic was much in demand. Troy Marion had been staying with the owner of a large tobacco farm fifty miles away and since he didn't own an automobile, Burl had been taking him to the farm on Sunday evenings and leaving him to stay all week and work for that owner. It was here he had met a young lady, the love of his life. Troy was in love and the family was going to meet her tonight.

The flat bed of the big truck allowed the riders to stretch out and have a space of their own and everyone seemed happy. When the truck turned from the main road onto the farm road, the girls said they wanted to get out of the cab and ride with the boys on the back. This would give everybody a chance to allow some cool air to pass along and through their clothes and make conditions better for all bodies. Burl could change gears in the truck without having one of the girls scoot over and sit on someone else's lap until the gear change was completed. The boys didn't seem to mind and invited their sisters to join them as they hung their feet over the edge of the truck bed. Two miles later, Burl braked the truck in front of a metal-roofed tobacco barn. The Marions were about to meet their future daughter-in-law.

A blue Ford tractor with a wooden wagon on four tires came wheeling around the back side of the barn somewhat faster than it ought to. The helms person at the command was Annabelle. She had black hair, considerable bulk and sporting a well-used pair of Carhart work pants. The driver operated the tractor-wagon combination like a pro and proved her prowess at being at home on the farm. She backed the rig into the barn without having to stop and correct any movement. All members of the Marion family stared speechless in admiration. Troy beamed. Burl rolled another cigarette. Annabelle strode over to meet everybody.

Set Another Place at the Table

After tobacco cutting season was over for another year, Annabelle became Mrs. Troy Marion and the young couple stayed on her father's farm. I didn't see either of them for over a year. They do return to the story later, however. Grand kids are fun.

The Chevrolet Truck

Earsel and Roy bought a used truck. One used truck for the boys to share equally and to serve each of them with their transportation needs. Willie was relating this information as we sat in their Chevrolet truck. It had been previously owned by someone who had manufactured a wooden bed with oak side boards. The transmission was the type that had a very low first gear referred to as the "bulldog" gear. With the combination of the flat, wooden bed and the low speed transmission, the truck had all the makings of a work truck. Top speed for such a vehicle was fifty five miles per hour.

Now that both boys were working at the same sawmill with the same schedule, there would be few problems with sharing the truck during the week. The trouble would come on Friday night and Saturday day and night when it would be decided who would get to use the automobile when and for how long.

Both boys had gotten their driver's license during the summer and the two were working all week and for the most part, things were going along nicely. Troy had moved away to another farm with his lovely lady Annabelle and occasionally, Earsel and Roy would drive down to see those two newlyweds. Annabelle had a sister. Her name was

Set Another Place at the Table

Madge and she was sixteen. When Earsel had his turn with the truck, he came to see Madge. When Roy could drive the truck, he came to see Madge.

Roy liked Madge but so did Earsel. Both the brothers had told Madge they loved her, but told her at different times. They had not told each other. Roy had bought her a scarf and Earsel had picked out a pretty broach for her to wear. Both young men had carried the gift in his pocket to keep it hidden until the moment of presentation. Each had intended to present this gift to her today.

Madge was playing to both men's fantasies and so was her father. Annabelle and Madge's father ran a large farm and was always needing help. He enjoyed seeing either boy come to visit with his daughter because they drove the Chevrolet truck with the flat bed. There were so many things to haul on the farm and the two boys were more than eager to please Madge's father. Both had been using their truck to work here. The low gear in the rig made it possible to travel at a speed slow enough for someone to walk alongside and throw bales of hay onto the boys vehicle. Today, the two Marion brothers came to visit their brother and his wife. Both Madge and Annabelle had learned to work on the farm just as if they had been boys and could handle any chore. Here in mid July, the focus was cutting, raking and baling hay to be taken to the big barns that were to be filled. Annabelle was excused from heavy lifting because she was expecting a child very soon so Madge spent a lot of time on the tractor performing these chores.

In one of these barns, Earsel and Roy found their girl high upon a loaded wagon throwing bales of hay to another person stationed in the barn loft. That person was a strong young man who smiled and flirted with Madge and she responded by giggling and giving him room to continue. The two were having so much fun flirting they had not seen the brothers come into the barn. Finally, the gentleman dropped down from the loft and the girl and guy disappeared from sight high atop a wagon load of fresh cut hay. Neither brother had much to say as they drove back home. Being jilted hurts a man's pride.

The boys continued to work on the farm during weekends but with pay this time. On the first Saturday in August of that year, both gentlemen were helping with another cutting of hay when Annabelle waddled into the barn and complained of labor pains. They were close together.

It was time for delivery and someone had to take her to the hospital. They climbed into the cab of the Chevrolet truck with the flat bed and the low geared transmission and headed to town. Top speed for a vehicle of this type is fifty to fifty five miles per hour. Willie told me later that his new niece was born on the stretcher before doctors could assist. Burl and May were grandparents.

Eighth Grade at Brickyard Elementary

Willie and I had a lady teacher in eighth grade. She was the wife of a preacher and a prim and proper woman. She had even less tolerance for misbehavior than other teachers. She had an understanding of how young boys and girls matured and how hormones ran amuck during these growing years. Willie was having major problems with acne, indigestion, body sweats and growth spurts. He was experiencing those problems when some body parts grow much faster than others. Willie's arms were so long he could not find room to fold them. His nose stuck out and so did his ears. His voice wouldn't say what he wanted to say unless he squeaked when he emphasized certain words and it happened when he didn't expect it. He was miserable but that didn't dampen his spirit to pester the girls.

Julie matured before the other girls in our class. She was pretty and a cheerleader for the basketball team. She had absolutely no interest or tolerance for Willie. He loved Julie. He loved her a little less after that day. She made it known to Willie that if he didn't leave her alone, she would "fix" him so he would never bother her again. He loved that attention and it spurred him on.

Eighth grade boys have gym class together with seventh

grade boys. During that period, the same combination of girls were having health class. There was a minute or two of transition when boys came back to the classroom and the girls were going to gym. It didn't matter if the teacher was looking or not, it happened. Cause and effect were demonstrated there in the hallway of Brickyard Elementary school. Willie never told me what he did to Julie but it was evident what Julie did for Willie. The smack could have been heard to the intersection and the groan that followed was heard through the hallways with the high ceilings all the way to the south end of the building which housed the lunchroom. Willie wore his tattoo for a long while. It was deeply imprinted in red across his left cheek. It was difficult to tell if puberty or the kick to his groin made him talk that way. He didn't care to bother Julie again. Our teacher never asked about the incident.

Mrs. Links

Shortly after the eighth grade school year began, Willie started leaving the classroom for short periods of time so he could be taught by another teacher named Mrs. Links. She was shorter than my friend and I thought it strange that Willie and she were having school somewhere else and not with us. She would come to our door and quietly ask Willie to come with her and later, he would return. My class was too busy to ask but we wondered why this was happening. We didn't talk about it if we sat together on the bus and I didn't ask. Mrs. Links seemed to care about students who had problems in the regular classroom and helped those who struggled to keep up with the rest of the class.

Mrs. Links played the piano for school functions such as cake walks, pie suppers and play programs that were held after school. Because she was short in stature, she required a thick, unabridged dictionary upon which to sit. Her feet barely touched the piano pedals but she played well. She also directed most of the programs that were held in the gym. She saw that Willie learned the necessary material to keep up with his lessons and he developed a deep respect for her.

She assigned to Willie the task of securing wooden canes for the Christmas play. He was more than happy to help his favorite teacher with the play. He also asked for my help getting enough canes for the wise men to use in their scenes. To do this task, the two of us took a walk into the woods to find tree limbs with natural crooks to be used for the props. Because of their relationship, he agreed to be a character in the play and wear an outfit depicting a wise man. No other teacher gave Willie this kind of attention. He had learned many other ways to get noticed. He earned the right to spend much time from gym class and recess and spent large amounts of time with the principal in his office. At times when Willie misbehaved to the point it became so severe, Mrs. Links was summoned to our room. She and Willie would leave together for a while. Willie learned that he could manipulate the system.

Christmas during eighth grade was memorable. The mature girls in my class could sing very well and performed for us every day. They learned Christmas songs and taught them to the reluctant boys. My part in the play was to recite some verses in the book of Luke from the Bible It was a long passage but I remember it still. Many parents came to the play to watch their kids and I remember Burl, an unlit, roll-your-own cigarette hanging from his mouth, watching with pride as Willie walked across stage and performed his parts.

Many years later after Willie had completed three years of military service and became a father to his own child, he visited Mrs. Links at her house. He went to tell her how much he appreciated the time she spent with him during his eighth grade class year.

Sue and Iris

There was just not enough money in the Marion household to spread among nine children and a couple of hungry dogs. As the two older girls became interested in trying to impress the boys at school, they found it impossible to be able to dress, primp or flirt the way other girls did. These two ladies were lucky if they had a change of clothes for the week. Of all the children, Sue and Iris spent the least amount of time at our house. There were times, however when my mom got involved in their teenage lives.

Living among siblings who found it necessary to compete for food and attention, the two growing girls held their own yet they were changing in many ways. At times they tried to acquire the traits and habits of other girls their age but found it difficult to break the mold which held them. Because there was no money for the things they saw other girls at school wear and carry, they had to improvise. My mom had also lived without many luxuries when growing up and had some ideas for the Marion girls to consider.

Sometimes on Sunday evening, my mom and the two girls would use our kitchen as a dressing room and experiment with hair styles, dresses, and at times, a little makeup. Mom could french-braid their hair and teach them how to do things along the line of cosmetics to help with appearance. Neither of the two girls were blessed with much natural beauty so most anything they did was an improvement. Their hearts, however, were good and knew that my mom did these things to try to help them. My sister would assist my mom when needed and even I could see the difference the attention made with the two emerging ladies.

With a pair of old scissors, mom would cut strips from a metal can that once contained commodity beef. Covering these strips with cloth, she made rollers for curling the girl's hair. Although both girls possessed naturally curly locks, these hand-made rollers left their hair with larger curls that looked better. In a few minutes, an old dress would be redone and fit one of the ladies like a new one. Mom used a sewing machine and cloth to work the miracles I saw evolve with the older Marion girls. While scurrying through the kitchen in search of a snack, I probably did a double take to see what a difference a little time and mom's ingenuity did with young ladies.

Mom was careful not to go too far with the beauty treatment and embarrass Sue and Iris. The next day was a school day and if the change in appearance was too drastic, fun would have been made at the expense of the two. It must have worked because school pictures from that time show the effort payed dividends for the young girls who grew up, found mates, and moved away.

Sue and Iris overcame the poverty and rough times at

home. Just as the green Studebaker car wore Ohio plates to the association of churches held near our home that summer, so did the automobiles owned by the future husbands of the two older Marion girls.

Uncle Sam Calls

During high school, Willie and I rode the same bus but were not as close friends as before. We had different interests and I believe he was struggling to make the grades necessary to stay in school. The girls, however, were there every day and made the best of the long ride to town on the school bus. The boys were always plaguing all the girls and trying to get anyone of them to pay attention to their silliness. Rosy was partially blind but didn't know it and had gotten a pair of glasses that increased her ability to see. It drastically improved her appearance for the better. Sue and Iris rode to school with their boyfriends in their cars. Blythe was still in grade school. Robert was sick and was confined to home health care.

In all animal kingdoms, pecking orders are established favoring the more dominant individuals. The same is true with children while riding on school buses. Donny was the dominant Alpha male. Rosy wanted to please him so she would do practically anything he would ask her to do. He sat with Rosy all the way home one day and worked with her psyche all the while. The task and target was Jimmy Jones who sat up front behind the driver. Donny asked her to kiss Jimmy on her way up the aisle before she got off the bus that afternoon. She was hesitant but Donny said he would kiss her right then and there if she would promise to carry out the task. He did and she did. The scene was rather amusing but caused quite a stir.

Burl was waiting at the bus stop the next morning and boarded the school bus. He rode the bus to Brickyard Elementary school and then on to the high school. Rosy sat with her father. I had never heard the bus that quiet before. Donny found a ride home with some friends.

These were good times but they were soon to end. The next year brought about drastic changes that affected our lives for years to come. The Viet Nam conflict began to escalate.

Soon after one's eighteenth birthday, a male was summoned to report for a physical examination at a city nearby. My friends boarded a chartered greyhound bus bound for Cattletsburg, Kentucky to be examined by a team of doctors to determine if they were physically fit to be a soldier. It was almost a sure bet one would be accepted. With a war being fought on another continent, few men were not found acceptable for service. Many households felt the pain and anxiety of having a son in the military. My brother received his draft papers and served much of his service time in Korea.

Roy received some papers in the mail and the Marion family came to our house to ask my dad to read them and explain what they meant. During supper my dad informed Burl and May that Roy needed to register for the draft. He had not done so and the police would come and get him if he didn't and they should do that soon. The papers were filled out at my house that evening after supper. A few weeks later, Uncle Sam called for Roy's services. Roy was sent to Viet Nam. The very next year, Troy was called but rejected because he and Annabelle had two children now. Soon after that, Earsel was called to service. He gave his life for his country and was buried in Crestline, Ohio.

My best friend Marvin received his letter from Uncle Sam about the same time and he too served his country by going to Viet Nam. It seemed that all my friends were getting the call and leaving. I was scared. I was not eighteen years old yet but the war was on everyone's mind and was the topic for evening news headlines. One of my school friends became the first casualty for my county. He received enemy fire while guarding his post. Willie Marion dropped out of high school and said he was going to join the army. He made a good soldier and served three years. He returned home and went to work with an electric company. Is it any wonder that his job was to use a mule to pull long strands of electrical wire from the top of one hill to another?

Upright and Ready!

A good friend named Gary taught a few guitar chords to me and had a lot of patience while I learned how to play a little. On Friday and Saturday nights, we played our instruments and sang for get-togethers at his house. We had similar interests and I rode in his hot rod car as a co-pilot and navigator. He dated and married a local girl and shortly after was drafted into the army. He and Willie were stationed at the same camp and became friends. They both wrote letters back home to keep me up to date as to what they were doing. They seemed so proud to be serving their country. Then one week there was no letter and I would not receive another from either of my friends. A year passed and I knew nothing of what or where they were or how they were doing. Gary's wife knew little more than I did.

One day, news came that Gary had been hurt and was in a hospital in Japan. Ninety days later, he came home to recuperate. When I heard that my friend was home from the army, I went to visit. I was naive to think we could take up where we left off with our previous relationship. I was ready to play guitar and sing and drag race again. Gary was not, however.

His wife met my friend and me at the door and asked us to be very quiet while she went to wake Gary. She had been trained how to approach her husband while he was sleeping. His army training had taught him to be "upright and ready" with a touch to his elbow. Deep inside the rainforests and jungles of South Vietnam, Gary existed because his training had taught him survival techniques that remained with him for a long time after his service time. Actually today flashbacks of those days come back to bother him. He hasn't said much about his experiences to me but he has touched on those events briefly in conversations. Gary remained in touch with Willie for years to come and their bond was broken only when Willie suffered a heart attack a few years ago.

Grandchildren Are Fun

After high school, Willie and I became separated and I didn't see him again for many years. He spent three years in military service. Upon leaving the military, he worked for a communications company and used his skills as a mule team driver to stretch long strands of wire across deep hollows in North Carolina, Tennessee and Kentucky. His family moved from the Marbury place and bought a small farm a few miles away.

I continued work toward a degree in education and secured a teaching position in a county school system nearby. After four years of teaching elementary students there, I transferred to another school in my own county system. In fact, I returned to Brickyard Elementary school to teach. It was interesting to see the new teachers who worked there and more remarkable, seeing a few of the very teachers who taught me when I went to school. What a difference a dozen years can make in one's appearance. My teachers looked older and so did I. They seemed glad to welcome me back to the old school as a member of the teaching staff. I received a lot of help and advice from the faculty. Work for me had started a week or so earlier and for good reasons. Teachers need this time to prepare for the opening day of school. I was unsure about how prepared I was. I read the list of names of the children who would be in my sixth grade class. Some were very familiar.

Sometimes no amount of preparation can get one ready for the initial shock of first meetings or first impressions. This was the situation which confronted me as I got acquainted with my class on that first day. I had a child with Marion as his last name. Troy and Annabelle Marion had a child in my class. Young John Marion had made time stand still and had nature produce a clone of his father. I laughed out loud when I saw the young lad . They had moved away from the farm and had come to this county to live near Burl and Mae. John looked up at me and grinned through his thin lips and said," My daddy knows you". I thought, "Yes, and I know your daddy".

Some things change while some things stay the same. I don't know what happened to the red Dodge truck with the flat bed but I somehow expected it to be driven up to the front of Brickyard Elementary to pick up John after school. It didn't come and John rode the school bus home every day. He came to school well dressed and clean. His gym shoes matched and his hair was cut by a professional barber, but he looked like his father.

I received my elementary school principal certification and became the school leader in a few years. By this time, several of the Marion grandchildren attended the school. Ironically, as good a job as Troy and Annabelle did keeping their son John in school, another brother did not do so well. In fact, as principal, I had to make many trips to this family's house to enforce the law regarding student punctuality and health issues. Finally, I won the confidence of the family and we started to make some progress. At other times, confrontations flared up between the mother of the children and me.

De JA Vu All Over Again

I didn't know what I wanted to do with my life after I finished high school. Uncle Sam was knocking at my door and I had prepared myself to go serve my country. I also wanted to go to college and that option became more attractive as weeks went by. With the help of scholarships awarded to me, I enrolled and completed four years and earned a Bachelor of Arts in Education. My first job was teaching elementary school in another county and I worked there for four years. My own county school system offered a job to me which meant I would be teaching in the same school I attended as a child. Brickyard Elementary had a position open for a sixth grade teacher. I accepted.

When a class roster was handed to me by the principal, I eagerly looked over the list to familiarize myself with my students. Two pupils whose last name was Marion appeared. Troy had moved next to his father, Burl. Roy had also moved a mobile home to the farm and lived in the school district. Each of them had fathered a child. Troy and Annabelle had produced a boy. Roy and his lady friend were raising a girl. I began teaching that year with an open mind.

My fifth year as a teacher was successful and the parents of my pupils were very supportive. They knew me as a child and felt a part of my classroom. The students respected me and found it interesting that their parents were my age. This year presented few problems.

Children grow up and attitudes change. Hormones run wild and this age group finds it difficult to accept the changes. This was the case with Burl's grand daughter, Loretta. She was an eighth grader and had given her father a mess of trouble. Skipping school, cursing her teacher, throwing items in the lunchroom, trashing the bathroom and striking other classmates were among the many misdemeanors she committed. She was out of control and the parents were notified several times about her troubles at school. Roy Marion was through with having to deal with his daughter and asked for a meeting with me after school to discuss what must be done to correct the situation.

Much like days of old, Roy sat outside in his truck and smoked while waiting for school to be dismissed. It had already been directed that she no longer could ride the school bus and Roy would need to come by and pick her up and take her home each day. Today, he came to school with hat in hand. He was to see first hand how his daughter, Loretta could misbehave.

The school bell rang and Loretta Marion burst from her classroom and ran toward the door that led to the playground. She sped full tilt and crashed into a much smaller child and knocked the student down to the floor. She never stopped running until she saw that I was waiting for her at the end of the sidewalk. Again, she couldn't stop quickly enough and plowed into me. She, in turn, landed on the sidewalk. Infuriated, she entered into a discussion with Satan himself and actually spoke his language fluently. Many of the expletives were directed toward me.

Roy witnessed all this and came to my rescue. Together, Roy, Loretta's mother, a flinching prematurely-developed hormonal daughter and an embarrassed teacher made their way to the principal's office. It may not have been the right thing to do but I shut the office door and waited outside in the hallway until father, mother and daughter worked things out to their satisfaction.

I felt like applauding. The screaming and cursing scorched the walls of the principal's office but attitudes were adjusted. It was just like old times again.

Important Papers

Burl Marion had the highest regard for my father. He looked up to Dad and put a lot of weight into what my dad told him. As far as Burl was concerned, the advice he got by coming to my house and talking with Dad was as good as he needed. Several times, he brought important documents to my home and asked Dad to read them aloud and explain what the words meant and tell him what he should do about the letter. For instance, Burl applied for a disability status and hoped the government would start sending him a monthly check. He had heard that all he needed to do was apply and the check was waiting. Dad explained that it wasn't so easy.

Another time the federal government cut the amount of subsidy given to tobacco growers. Yet another time, the tobacco acreage allowed to farmers was cut. One time he had not paid the taxes on his truck and would have to pay a late penalty. . All these papers arrived in the mail and somehow the Marions knew which envelopes contained the important papers and which did not. There was on time when the importance of the mail correspondence could be questioned.

In an important-looking manila package, a picture of a

good-looking female and a letter arrived stating the need for a proper American family to help this young lady find a home. She was a hard worker and could give references to support her claim. Troy had corresponded with the lady and she was to arrive in a few days. Burl wanted my dad to help his son get out of this mess. Dad didn't want to get involved in anything like this. He did, however suggest that no money be sent to anyone and maybe she wouldn't come if her trip was not financed. The lady did not make it to this part of America.

Some good news came, however, about a year later. Burl's first Social Security check with back pay came in the mail. He was proud of this brown envelope and brought it to show Dad. The two of them took a long walk up the hollow. I don't know what transpired between the two men but I think my dad suggested that he start a bank account and deposit future checks into the account on the very day it arrived. Dad probably explained that money is much safer in a bank than at home. I can only guess about that part of the conversation. Burl and Mae moved from the farm and bought some land a few miles away. They had a source of income now and life would be better.

Burl and Mae took a ride everyday in the big red Dodge truck. It seemed that she sat much closer to her husband than before. Mom said her hair looked to be much fuller but shorter. The sleeve of his new white shirt showed as they drove with the truck window rolled down. Both smoked a cigarette and laughed out loud as they turned onto the dirt road that led up the hollow to the Marion house. Only Rosy was living at home and she didn't like to ride in the truck anymore. There was no need to plow and prepare large areas of land and no reason to raise crops to eat. The government took care of them. Rosy's check was small but came to the mailbox as regularly as the phases of the moon.

The Last Chapter

The fifty-seven Chevrolet is several decades old but has more value today than when it rolled from the assembly line. One can see a few of these classics from time to time in car shows and in magazines which feature older cars. Families have more than one color television with hundreds of choices of stations to surf through with the remote control. There is a constant chatter from those who use cell phones that are small enough to hide in the palm of your hand. One doesn't have to ask permission to use a neighbor's rotary phone and have an entire community listen to your conversation. The only place one could find an outhouse is at a construction site and they are all painted blue and smell pretty good. Times, they are a-changin'.

The make-believe family who played the major parts in my story still live through their great-grandchildren. I think I would recognize them as being descendants of Burl and Mae by some quaint action or automatic body movement they wouldn't know they performed. I believe I would know their great grandparents through the eyes and smiles of the children.

There are more incidents and episodes that come to mind and could have happened if I should choose to write them down. I won't because my sides are still hurting after re-reading this story. Please feel free to read it again for yourself.

These eight years provided enough time for children to grow into adolescents and teenagers to young men and women. Some of them married and had children of their own. We know about them and their lifestyles, but what about the things we don't know? Did Rosy ever get glasses or modern day surgery for her eyes? How did Earsel die? Who did the older girls marry? What happened to the mule? Where did Uncle Raymond get to spend his time? What was this uncle carrying in his suitcases?

Today, great grandchildren of Burl and Mae could be old enough to be attending some school far away. Do the window shades need adjusting? Do the chalk trays need emptying? How much does a school lunch cost? Are they still serving hamburgers?

Grandpa's
Medicine Bottles

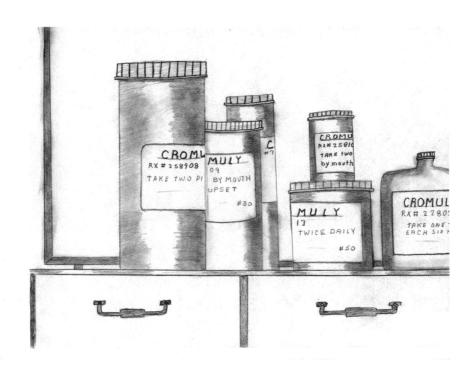

Grandpa didn't take his medicine this morning. It sits there on the dresser in the little bottles of various sizes with direction stickers on each. It has sat this way for months, probably so Grandpa won't get it mixed up. Several times, as I pass his room, I have noticed and it wasn't important then. But now, without him lying there in bed, I paid particular attention to the bottles all in a row, some small, some tall. Grandpa sure has a lot of medicine!

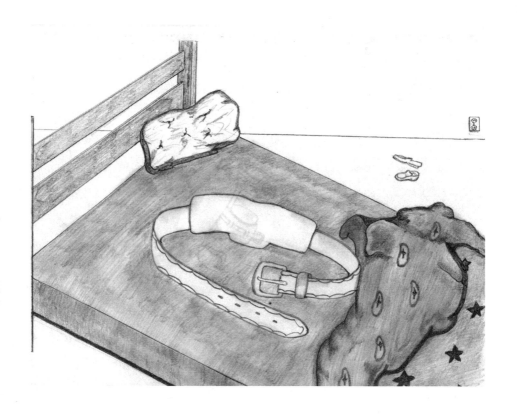

Grandpa couldn't stand much noise and I couldn't run my battery-powered fire engine near his room. It was a different kind of quiet now. It was almost like the time I had an earache and mom put a cotton ball in my left ear. Sounds were so far away and the smell of medicine was so near. It was much like that at this moment while I stood in the doorway and looked at an empty bed. Do you want to see me place my hands against either side of the door and push myself up and hang with my feet off the floor?

I was doing that when I remembered that I had overheard some strange man say that Grandpa had "gone to meet his maker". Wherever that was, he would have to borrow a back brace because the one Grandpa wore was lying there on his unmade bed.

Grandpa never played baseball with me. Grandma did. She was so funny when she threw the ball back to me. She used the wrong foot to push from and I told her and even tried to show her but she never learned. She never played for long, either, because she had to go back inside to check on Grandpa. Grandma was stronger than Grandpa. She could lift him up in bed and even turn him over when he grumbled about how much he hurt. I have seen her get up in bed with him and adjust the brace around his back by placing her knee against him and pulling the leather straps. Those straps are not fastened now. They lie there as if waiting for him to return.

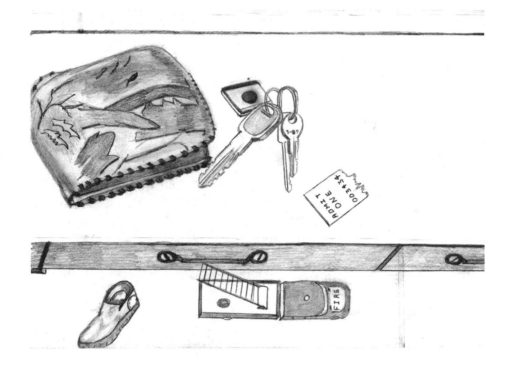

134

Everybody went with Grandpa except my big brother. We share a room. He doesn't get up from his bed til late in the day either. He doesn't take any medicine so there are no bottles, tall or small, on our dresser. His car keys, his wallet and a ticket stub from the movie house are all that I saw when I looked earlier. Greg plays baseball with me but he throws the ball too fast and it hurts when I catch it. I wonder if Grandpa hurts like I do? I wondered if someday I would have to wear a back brace too? Greg would know where Grandpa went and how long my mother would be gone. My brother likes it quiet while he sleeps so I can't use my battery-powered tooth brush now.

Rags got free from her leash one time and jumped into bed with Grandpa. She licked him over and over until Grandma pulled her onto the floor and swatted her behind with the straw broom. My mom shut the door quickly so I could not hear what was being yelled but later she and Grandma said that Grandpa had to "vent" occasionally and he really vented that time! Do you want to see me chin myself by reaching my arms above my head and jumping up to grab the board over the door and pulling myself up? I was doing this when I thought about how I enjoyed playing with Rags and I didn't mind when she licked me. Her breath smelled like dog food and that wasn't bad. She doesn't like to get near the broom anymore. I wonder if she knows Grandpa is not here?

Grandpa's medicine bottles look like city buildings, some tall, some small. Their reflection in the glass mirror makes them look real. Mom knows which medicine is in which bottle and how much and when and what for and all that stuff only doctors usually know. She has never said "Don't go into Granpa's room." I just don't. Do you want to see me lie down on the floor inside the door and scoot my feet way up the wood on the sides? I'm almost upside down! Actually, as I look around Grandpa's room, everything looks that way. Grandma says my face gets red when I do that and she laughs with me. She's a cool grandma but she went with Grandpa today. Grandma always has to take care of him. She'll play baseball with me when she gets back.

Grandpa's medicine bottles look like Mom's spice rack. Some are small, some are tall. Grandpa sure takes a lot of medicine!

About the Author

Sandy Knipp earned a Bachelor's Degree in Education from Morehead State University in 1971, a Master of Arts in Education in 1974 and a Rank I in Administration in 1981. He taught elementary school and served as principal until he retired in 1988. On March 4, 1999, he received a kidney transplant from a close friend who had passed on.

Today, he uses his musical talents to write, play and sing many different kinds of song. He plays guitar, bass and banjo as he works with the public outreach component of the Kentucky Center for Traditional Music. Mr. Knipp reads to audiences from original pieces and Kentucky authors. One other work written and illustrated by Knipp is entitled, "Grandpa's Medicine Bottles" and has been read to hundreds of students in eastern Kentucky. He was awarded the "Appalachian Treasure Award" by Morehead State University in 2002. He is married and has three children and three grandchildren.